# 50 FINDS OF EARLY MEDIEVAL COINAGE FROM THE PORTABLE ANTIQUITIES SCHEME

John Naylor

AMBERLEY

*For Mum and Dad*

First published 2021

Amberley Publishing
The Hill, Stroud
Gloucestershire, GL5 4EP

www.amberley-books.com



ISBN 978 1 4456 9532 7 (print)
ISBN 978 1 4456 9533 4 (ebook)



British Library Cataloguing in Publication Data.
A catalogue record for this book is available from the British Library.

Typeset in 10pt on 13pt Celeste.
Typesetting by SJmagic DESIGN SERVICES, India.
Printed in the UK.

# Contents


| | | |
|---|---|---|
| | Acknowledgements | 4 |
| | Foreword | 5 |
| | Introduction | 6 |
| 1 | The End of Roman Britain to the Early Medieval Kingdoms: Fifth to Mid-seventh Centuries | 8 |
| 2 | The Rise of Silver: Mid-seventh to Mid-ninth Centuries | 25 |
| 3 | From the Viking Age to the Norman Conquest: *c.* 880–1066 | 68 |
| | Further Reading | 96 |

# Acknowledgements

This book has been built on the work of many people, the '50 Finds' recorded and identified by PAS staff, their interns and volunteers, sometimes with additional information from other specialists. In alphabetical order, they are: Kurt Adams, Jo Ahmet, David Algar, Martin Allen, Liz Andrews-Wilson, Frank Basford, Edward Besly, Angie Bolton, Anna Booth, Andrew Brown, Laura Burnett, Charlotte Burrill, Anni Byard, Helena Costas, Adam Daubney, Lucy Ellis, Simon Holmes, Becky Griffiths, Ciorstaidh Hayward Trevarthen, Richard Henry, Katie Hinds, Gail Hitchens, Kevin Leahy, Mark Lodwick, Adrian Marsden, Caroline McDonald, Sam Moorhead, Richard Morrissey, Vanessa Oakden, Andrew Rogerson, Anja Rohde, Wendy Scott, Kate Sumnall, Luke Treadwell, Anna Tyacke, Emily Tilley, Julian Watters, Rob Webley, Henry Weeds, David Williams, Gareth Williams, Andrew Woods and Danielle Wootton. Each record can be found on the PAS database (finds.org.uk/database). These records form the basis for each entry and are used to illustrate aspects of coin use in the early medieval world. These broader discussions would not have been possible without the hard work by all PAS staff past and present recording and identifying large numbers of objects from across England and Wales, enabling me to discuss the coinage and its circulation in the countryside in a way that would not otherwise have been possible. They all deserve my thanks. Thanks also to all of the finders who voluntarily offer their finds for recording; every one helps to build a bigger picture. The images of coins from the Watlington Hoard came from the Ashmolean Museum, Oxford, and I would like to thank them for their permission to use these. Needless to say, responsibility for errors or omissions in this book are mine alone. On a personal note, my thanks as ever to Heather, Sam and Maggie for pretty much everything else.

# Foreword

The Portable Antiquities Scheme has been one of the heritage success stories of the last twenty years, and sets a standard internationally. It aims to systematically record archaeological objects found by members of the public throughout England and Wales. This great project has engaged with thousands of people – many of them metal detectorists – enabling them to report their discoveries responsibly. These finds have made a significant contribution to archaeological research at a local, regional and national level, not least by providing a geographical coverage impossible through archaeological excavation alone. As I write, the PAS has just reached the milestone of recording 1.5 million finds, an impressive testimony to the success of the venture. The Ashmolean Museum's involvement with the PAS began in 2004. Since then it has hosted the Scheme's National Finds Adviser for Early Medieval and Later Coinage, a post which John has held since 2007. Like many museums around the country our collections now include important finds recorded by the PAS – some reported under the Treasure Act 1996 – from single items to large hoards. The most notable hoard is the nationally important Watlington Hoard, which makes a direct contribution to the narrative history of our country. Most of the objects recorded by the PAS, however, and many of those discussed in this book, are more representative of the everyday experience of life in the past. Together these objects help us to understand more fully the histories of the people who lived here before us.

John has thanked others in the Acknowledgements but he himself deserves our thanks. The Finds Liaison Officers of the Portable Antiquities Scheme, and through them the finders of the objects reported, rely on John's training, support and expertise. This book presents some of the highlights and insights of their combined efforts.

Prof Chris Howgego
Keeper of the Heberden Coin Room
Ashmolean Museum
Oxford

# Introduction

Every year the Portable Antiquities Scheme (PAS) records tens of thousands of objects dating from the Palaeolithic to the twentieth century which have been found by members of the public. Among them are objects from the early medieval period — around 4,000 in an average year, coins accounting for about 500 of these — which spans the six-and-a-half centuries from the end of Roman Britain in around AD 410 until the Norman Conquest in 1066. These finds have had a major impact on archaeological research and, combined with the accurate recording of findspots, we can now research the countryside and provide detailed context for archaeological excavations that was simply unavailable before. Early medieval coins are the focus of this book and a great example of how PAS-recorded finds make a vital contribution to broader archaeological research.

Most coins that the PAS record were probably lost by accident and these are reported to us voluntarily by their finders; some others, finds converted into jewellery or buried in hoards for example, have to be declared by law under the Treasure Act 1996. Many of these end up in museum collections after the payment of a reward that is divided between the finder and the landowner. The finds in this book reflect both of these pathways to recording, although the majority that I've used to tell the story of early medieval coinage are stray finds voluntarily reported to the PAS by their finders.

What all finds have in common, though, is that they belonged to someone. The 'lives' of these objects – archaeologists call this 'object biography' – were also varied. After they were made, they could have been given, received, spent, stored, changed, loved, dismissed, stolen and so on; at some point they were lost, discarded or buried, only to be rediscovered in the present day. Each and every one tells us something about its past. It might come from a settlement or a cemetery, a monastery, market place or a roadway; it may have been lost one day in the fields or dumped along with midden waste cleaned from a settlement. Put together, especially with the evidence from archaeological excavations, a picture of how people lived can be constructed.

Coins, like all other archaeological objects, have their particular histories too. Importantly they represent the authority that produced them. This could be the king (and the state), the Church, local aristocracy or even merchants, and at their simplest coins are economic objects, stores of wealth whose value can be trusted. Their issuers, though, may have been as interested in spreading messages about themselves or their beliefs as in producing a piece of money, so coins are adorned with images and iconography that might relate to kingship, religion and identity. Coins do the same today; just look at the ones in your pocket. Their use also reflects the people who owned them, using them in all sorts of ways from the expected (coins as money, used to buy, sell or store wealth) to the unexpected (as jewellery or amulets for example). Each of the fifty finds in this book explores something of these topics, sometimes more than one, and follows some of the stories which together can tell the varied and interesting history of coinage in early medieval Britain from a society without a functioning coin-based economy for much of the fifth century to one with a complex, well-respected, multi-denominational coinage by the time of the Norman Conquest in 1066.

As in any subject, the study of coins – numismatics – has its own set of terminology, some of which inevitably crops up in the pages that follow. These are worth briefly discussing and explaining here. A good place to start are the terms 'obverse' and 'reverse'. The obverse of a coin is best thought of as the 'heads' of a coin, the reverse its 'tails'. These terms also normally tell us something about coin production. Coins were struck by hand, the designs engraved or stamped onto dies. One die was secured in place, the other held and struck with a hammer to stamp the designs onto a blank piece of metal, the flan. The lower die is normally the obverse, the hand-held die the reverse. This is a useful convention to use when studying dies. There were usually more reverse than obverse dies because they absorbed most of the force of each hammer blow and were more likely to be damaged more quickly.

The character of the 'moneyer' is also discussed quite regularly in this book, and often named too. This was the person who oversaw the production of coinage – its minting – and took responsibility for it, quite often having their name incorporated into the inscription, normally on the reverse of the coin. Moneyers worked at a 'mint' although, in practice, this was more likely a collection of workshops in this period all run by individual moneyers, and some moneyers probably moved around, especially for the coinage discussed in the earlier parts of this book up until the middle of the eighth century. The name of the mint is regularly included on coins from the later tenth century.

My hope in writing this book is to show how coins – in this case early-medieval coins – have much to tell us about the people and societies who produced them, and that they were far more than just 'money in your pocket' for use in buying and selling. If this book sparks an interest in wanting to know more about life in the early medieval period it will have done its job and I've included a few pointers for further reading at the end.

# Chapter 1
# The End of Roman Britain to the Early Medieval Kingdoms: Fifth to Mid-seventh Centuries

The two centuries following the end of the Roman administration in Britain are complex and important. The fifth and sixth centuries saw the migration of people across the North Sea, the extent and scope of which archaeology has shown was regionally varied. The fourth–sixth centuries in western Britain show greater levels of continuity and there was minimal influence from the Germanic styles seen in central, southern and eastern England. By the seventh century the Roman province of Britannia had been replaced by competing kingdoms with some, like Mercia and Northumbria, already powerful. These emerging elites can be seen from the late sixth century in palaces and estate centres, and in rare but often extravagant 'princely' graves, such as the famous ship burial at Sutton Hoo in Suffolk. The seventh century is also a period of conversion after the adoption of Christianity over the older, pagan beliefs held previously, although in western Britain Christianity had been present throughout. This brought rulers into the orbit of the Church and other Christian rulers in Europe and the Mediterranean.

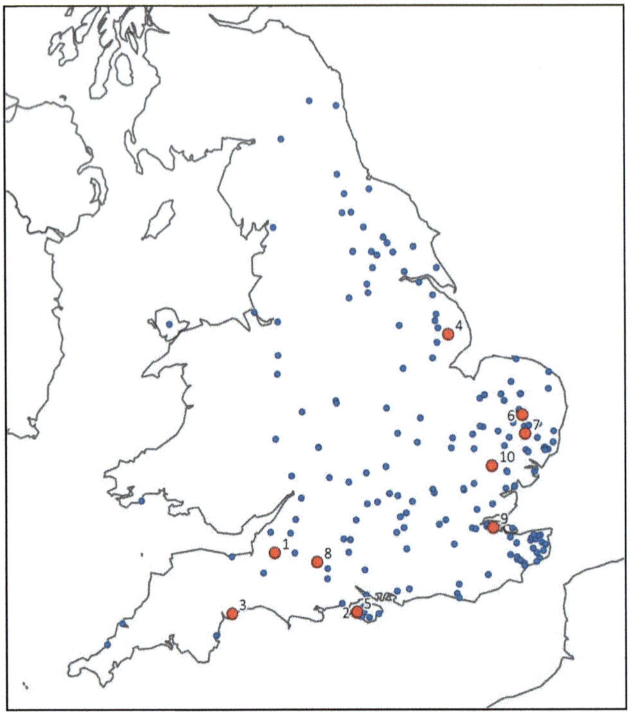


Map of PAS-recorded coin finds dating *c.* 410–670 and showing the location of Finds 1–10.

**1. Clipped silver *siliqua*, 395–402, from St Cuthbert Out, Somerset (SOM-5CED37)**
Diameter: 13 mm.

Every year the PAS records a number of late Roman silver *siliquae* that have been clipped around the edges. This example, probably in the name of the Emperor Valens (364–378), was likely minted around 367–375. It has been severely clipped, leaving the coin irregularly shaped and much smaller than it was originally. The clipping has effectively removed the inscription on the obverse, leaving only the ruler's head, and on the reverse the top and bottom parts of the design which shows Roma seated holding a Victory on a globe and a spear. The clipping of *siliquae* appears to be a phenomenon of the first half of the fifth century, the silver removed to stretch supplies while maintaining some form of circulating currency, reaching the point that some *siliquae* only survive as chopped-up fragments of bullion. Recognising that coins like this one were clipped during the fifth century is important. It highlights that Roman Britain did not suddenly end in AD 410 and that change in many places was slow, continuing the transformations that had been occurring for some time already.

Clipped *siliqua* of Honorius from St Cuthbert Out, Somerset (SOM-5CED37).

Unclipped *siliqua* of Arcadius dating to 388–402 (WILT-7B0682).

Chopped-up *siliquae* (BERK-B57B97; HAMP-3A1712).

**2. Pierced copper-alloy Roman *nummus*, *c*. 335–41, from Shalfleet, Isle of Wight (IOW-51FADA)**
Diameter: 18.7 mm; weight: 2.34 g.

Pierced Roman *nummi* dating from the second–fourth centuries are not uncommon finds in fifth–seventh-century graves. This worn coin of the House of Constantine is quite typical, pierced to the left of the Emperor's head. It was found in an area on the Isle of Wight that may have been the site of a cemetery. Excavations of such cemeteries in England show that pierced Roman coins were often worn as pendants on necklaces, although they are also sometimes found in bags buried with the deceased. They are most commonly buried in the graves of women. It is unlikely that these coins were Roman-period keepsakes or heirlooms but were found and reused in the fifth–seventh centuries. We cannot know what their use on necklaces and in burials may have meant to people at the time, whether it was simply an attractive form of decoration or had a deeper meaning, perhaps as some form of amulet or a perceived link to the past.

Pierced *nummus* from Shalfleet, Isle of Wight (IOW-51FADA).

## 3. A hoard of four Byzantine copper *folles*, sixth century, from Bicton, Devon (DEV-464726)

Until recently it was thought that most British finds of copper-alloy coins from Byzantium, the Eastern Roman Empire ruled from Constantinople (Istanbul, Turkey), were modern losses brought back by travellers or soldiers. Recent research has shown that some did reach Britain in the fifth–seventh centuries, their dark green surface patina very different to the yellowish buff colour of most of the Mediterranean finds. This hoard of four coins, found near the East Devon coast, is a good example. Dating to the reigns of emperors Justin I (518–27) and Justinian I (527–65), their findspot is inland from the coast behind High Peak where excavations uncovered a large enclosure and fifth–sixth-century finds. These include pottery made in the Mediterranean, showing that the area had long-distance trade links. The coins found at Bicton support the idea that sites like High Peak had direct contact with Mediterranean traders. There are Byzantine *folles* from other coastal areas in south-west and western Britain and archaeologists have excavated other sites like High Peak with Mediterranean links, including Bantham (Devon) and Tintagel (Cornwall).

Two copper *folles* from a hoard of Byzantine coins from Bicton, Devon (DEV-464726).

## 4. Merovingian gold *solidus*, mid–late sixth century, from the Louth area, Lincolnshire (BM-EE0045)

Diameter: 21 mm; weight: 4.43 g.

This gold *solidus* is a typically Byzantine coin. The figure on the obverse wears a helmet and armour, and holds an orb with a cross on top, a *globe cruciger*. On the reverse is an angel – the old Imperial Victory – standing with a cross in one hand and *globe cruciger* in the other. The inscription includes the name IVSTINIANVS, identifying the ruler as Justinian I (527–65). However, the style is quite crude, the face of the Emperor and the standing figure not very clear. The inscription is difficult to read. This is because the coin is not an official Byzantine issue but was produced by the Merovingians, one of the Germanic groups ruling in post-Roman western Europe. Their territory included what is now southern France where this coin was struck, and is a typical sixth-century issue. Known as 'pseudo-Imperial' because they copy official Imperial coins, they are found in small numbers in Britain. It is likely that many of those imported here would have ended up melted down to produce gold jewellery and other items.

Merovingian *solidus* from the Louth area, Lincolnshire (BM-EE0045).

Pendant produced from Gallic 'pseudo-Imperial' *solidus* in the name of Maurice Tiberius, 582–602 (KENT-AC7E52).

Sixth-century 'pseudo-Imperial' *tremisses* of King Gundomar, 524–32 (SF-A84316), and from the Lower Rhine (KENT-E4979A), both copying issues of Justinian I.

**5. Visigothic gold *tremissis*, mid–late sixth century, from Shalfleet, Isle of Wight (IOW-715794)**
Diameter: 12.9 mm; weight: 1.47 g.

The Visigoths settled in southern France and Spain from the early–mid fifth century, this coin originating in the latter. Imitating a Byzantine *tremissis* of Justinian I (527–65), it has a right-facing bust on the obverse and a winged Victory advancing right on the reverse, but the designs have become abstract and devolved. The Victory is now almost insect-like with too many legs, a strangely shaped head and the inscription just a series of motifs made from wedges. Even the cross on the chest, a quite common element of Visigothic *tremisses*, is barely recognisable. Visigothic objects are rare finds in Britain with around thirty-five recorded by the PAS, including buckles and belt mounts alongside coins. The largest group comes from the Isle of Wight, possibly a group of coins dispersed from a grave, and the thin distribution hugs the coast from the Solent to North Yorkshire. These concentrations of finds highlight the very active zones of contact on either side of the English Channel and southern North Sea.

Visigothic *tremissis* from Shalfleet, Isle of Wight (IOW-715794).

Fifth-century 'pseudo-Imperial' Visigothic coinage in the name of Roman Emperors Severus III, 461–5, (OXON-5E3E68) and Zeno, 474–91 (KENT-B34CC4).

A lyre-shaped Visigothic buckle found at Martin, Lincolnshire (LIN-F3054B).

**6. Coin pendants, 636–59, from Winfarthing, Norfolk (NMS-E95041)**
Coin with attached loop dimensions: 19.9x24.4 mm; weight: 4.27 g
Coin with detached loop diameter of coin: 19.4x25.2 mm; weight: 4.16 g

The inclusion of gold or silver coins in graves was a regular, if minor, element of the fifth–seventh-century burial rite. The two coins here are gold *solidi* of the Merovingian ruler Sigebert III (636–59) minted in Marseilles (France). They were struck from the same set of coin dies – so the coins are called 'die-linked' – and at some point were converted into pendants through the addition of a gold loop to the top of each coin. The die-linking means that the coins were not just plucked from the circulating currency for conversion into jewellery but had never entered general circulation in the first place. They were found on a necklace in a very rich woman's grave, which was archaeologically excavated after its initial discovery by a metal detectorist. The woman's body was adorned with high-quality gold jewellery and silver items, and a copper-alloy bowl, a knife and imported pottery were also found. This suggests that she was a member of an elite local family. Gold coins are found in both male and female graves, being converted into pendants in female burials but left unmodified for males. These are usually very high status – a purse of gold coins was found in the royal ship burial at Sutton Hoo – and are part of a suite of objects that represent wealth and power, linking to the burgeoning networks of international trade which appeared during the seventh century.

Coin pendants made from *solidi* of Sigebert III from a burial at Winfarthing, Norfolk (NMS-E95041).

**7. Merovingian gold *tremissis*, *c.* 580–670, from Wetheringsett-cum-Brockford, Suffolk (SF-F3F683)**
Diameter: 13.4 mm; weight: 1.26 g.

The most commonly found coins of the late sixth and seventh centuries are gold *tremisses* produced by the Merovingians after around 580, their value equivalent to a third of a *solidus*. The designs are quite consistent, most with a bust on the obverse and a cross motif on the reverse, and inscriptions naming the mint place and the moneyer, an official in charge of the production of the coin. This coin was struck at the Northern French port of Quentovic, located near the mouth of the River Canche and one of the most important trading places in northern Europe at the time. It was minted by the moneyer Dutta. Like many finds of *tremisses* in Britain it was found relatively close to the coast, showing the importance of maritime trade to the use of these coins. Only around a dozen or so Merovingian coins are reported to the PAS each year, every one an important find. Long-term recording has shown patterns in their distribution, emphasising how coin use in south-east England and East Anglia developed earlier than in other places during the seventh century.

Merovingian *tremissis* from Wetheringsett-cum-Brockford, Suffolk (SF-F3F683).

Examples of Merovingian *tremisses* recorded by the PAS. Top: BH-9B6B89 (mint: Orléans, France; moneyer: Angliulfus); bottom: IOW-C42F03 (mint: Senlis, France; moneyer: Ursoleni).

Top: HAMP-38D124 (mint: Rodez, France); bottom: LIN-0B3EEB (Nietap type).

**8. Gold shilling of 'Witmen-derived' type, *c.* 620–45, from Stockton, Wiltshire (DOR-C0552F)**
Diameter: 11.7 mm; weight: 1.29 g.

Gold shillings (also known as '*thrymsas*') were equivalent to the Merovingian *tremissis*. Minting started around the turn of the seventh century in south-east England, although they were not produced in large numbers or many different types until the 620s. This coin is based on a unique coin whose inscription reads WITMEN MONITA, and has a design comparable to the Merovingian *tremisses*. On the obverse, there is a right-facing bust with a trident-like motif in front, and the reverse has a central cross with the now-illegible inscription around the outside. This type forms the main part of the Crondall Hoard, buried in the 640s in Crondall, Hampshire, the largest hoard of seventh-century gold coins found in England. Their generally high gold content, around 50–70 per cent, places them in the earlier phases of the gold coins and they are mostly found south of the River Thames, although there is another contemporary group probably struck at York. This example is the most south-westerly find of a shilling recorded by the PAS. Shillings dating to this 'Crondall Hoard' phase of the coinage are extremely rare finds, the PAS having recorded fewer than ten to date, suggesting they enjoyed only limited circulation albeit over a wide area.

Gold shilling of 'Witmen-derived' type from Stockton, Wiltshire (DOR-C0552F).

Gold shilling of the 'York group' from Fulford, near York dating to *c.*. 620–45 (YORYM-504283).

Gold shilling of 'Cross-Cross' type, the only other 'Crondall hoard' type recorded by the PAS (ESS-3263B5)

## 9. Gold *solidus* pendant, *c.* 635–45, from the Hoo peninsula, Kent (KENT-5E6A92)

Dimensions: 19.5x18.5 mm; weight: 3.2 g.

Alongside shillings *solidi* were occasionally produced, this find being a rare example. The design is influenced by earlier coinage, its obverse copying the style of late fourth-century Roman issues (compare to the *solidus* pictured in Find 10) and the reverse a 'cross-on-steps' type introduced by the Byzantine Emperor Heraclius (610–41). This helps to broadly date the coin and its gold content to around 635–45. Five finds of this coin type are known, all modified into pendants with the loop broken on this example. This must make us ask whether they were intended to be used as coins or were simply coin-like jewellery. The gold content of one example was analysed and it was discovered that the loop contained a different amount of gold to the coin. This suggests it was modified at a different time to its striking, supporting the idea that it is a coin. Only one other example has a findspot, also in Kent, and it is likely that they were produced in this region.

Pendant made using a *solidus* from the Hoo peninsula, Kent (KENT-5E6A92).

Byzantine *solidus* of Heraclius with reverse type copied on Find 9 (DUR-EBAF01).

**10. Gold shilling, *c.* 645–70, from Castle Hedingham, Essex (LEIC-E1C167)**
Diameter: 12 mm; weight: 1.21 g.

Later shillings contain more silver than the earlier issues and they are often referred to as 'pale gold', reflecting the effect of this increasing silver content on their colour. The largest group are the 'Two Emperors' type, a stylised copy of a late Roman gold *solidus*, showing two seated emperors on the reverse with a winged Victory above. The shillings, though, were produced on a much smaller flan and so only a part of the design was copied. Their gold content varies between about 20 and 50 per cent suggesting the 'Two Emperors' was a long-lived type and the style changes little implying that their production was well-regulated. PAS-recorded finds have a tight distribution from Norfolk to Kent, a core area of circulation and one highlighting an early monetized zone. The coin is also pierced showing it was adapted to be worn as a pendant, an increasingly rare modification by this time as coin use increased.

Pierced 'Two Emperors' shilling from Castle Hedingham, Essex (LEIC-E1C167).

Top: A late Roman 'Two Emperors' *solidus* of Gratian, AD 368–83 (DENO-75191A); bottom: 'pale gold' phase shilling of 'concordia/clasped hands' type (WILT-DEDC91).

'Pale gold' phase shillings of 'Crispus' type (SF-421DCA) and 'Constantine' type (SF-4AA4E3).

# Chapter 2
# The Rise of Silver: Mid-seventh to Mid-ninth Centuries

This period can be seen as the time when a few large kingdoms dominated much of what is now England. Mercia (the Midlands) was the most powerful for much of this time, having control over the east and south of the country, including the kingdoms of East Anglia and Kent. Wessex consolidated its control in the south and south-west, and Northumbria controlled lands north of the Humber as far as southern Scotland. It was also a period when international trade, across the English Channel and around the North Sea, blossomed and large, town-like ports became centres for craft working and exchange. From the late eighth century the Vikings became a serious threat, and by the 870s had conquered kingdoms and raided much of the country.

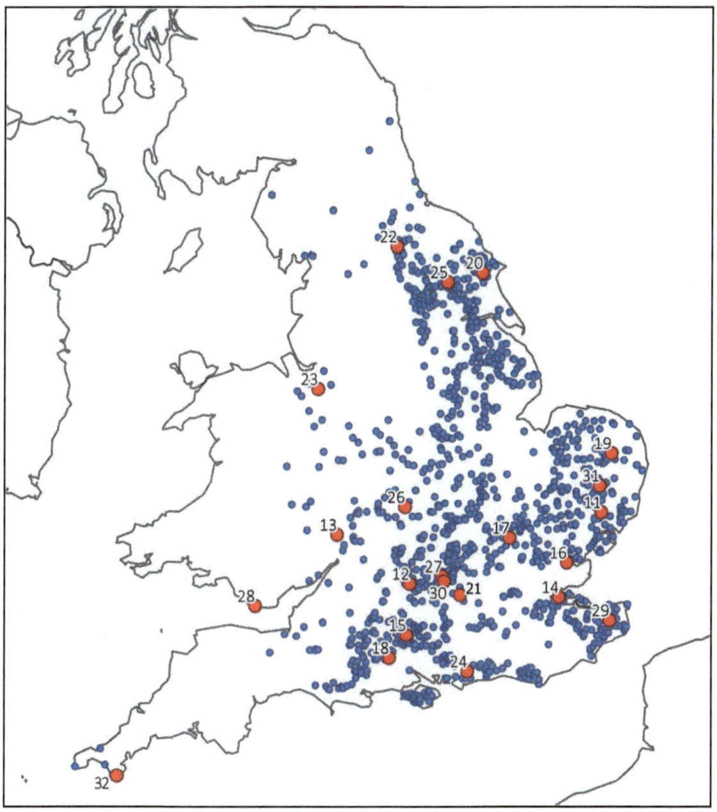


Map of PAS-recorded coin finds dating *c.* 665/70–*c.* 879 and showing the location of Finds 11–32.

## 11. A Pre-Primary Phase *sceat* of Series Pa, *c.* 665–75, from Barham, Suffolk (SF-0C2A17)

Diameter: 13 mm; weight: 1.23 g.

In the 660s the final transition from gold to silver coinage took place. This change seems to have been a deliberate move towards a lower value coin for use in the trade networks around the North Sea. These coins, struck on small, thick flans, were produced until the middle of the eighth century, are commonly called *sceattas*, and can be thought of as early pennies. Numismatists have divided the enormous numbers of designs into 'series' of related types from which two chronological phases – the Primary and Secondary – have been discerned, the division in the years around 710. This coin is one of two types belonging slightly earlier than most Primary Phase coins; the type was initially pale gold and ended production as silver. It has the word 'pada' in runes on the reverse, which might be the name of a moneyer. The runes are within a rectangular standard, although either the standard or the inscription is upside down, and the obverse bust wears an elaborate crested helmet, a symbol of power and authority. The coin came from a site with wide-ranging contacts in the seventh century, only to decline after nearby Ipswich expanded greatly in the early eighth century. *Sceattas* are the most commonly found early medieval coins with around 150 recorded by the PAS each year, a figure not reached again until the eleventh century. Their introduction coincides with a period of vibrant international and regional trade, and their widespread distribution shows that more people were using coins in transactions.

Series Pa *sceat* from Barham, Suffolk (SF-0C2A17).

A Pre-Primary Phase *sceat* of Series Va with inscription spelling Vanimundus (IOW-E09AAE).

**12. A silver *sceat* of Primary Phase Series A, *c.* 670–90, from East Challow, Oxfordshire (BERK-220047)**
Diameter: 12 mm; weight: 1.2 g.

This coin of Series A belongs early in the Primary Phase. It was probably minted in Kent, one of the main areas for early coin use as we saw for the gold coins. It was found in Oxfordshire, a little outside of this zone but one where excavations of sixth–seventh-century cemeteries have shown links to Kent. The design uses a range of elements from earlier coinage on both obverse and reverse, including the crown, bust shape and inscriptions. A long-lived issue, Series A slowly devolves through three types (A1–A3; this coins is an A2) but with little real design change. It, in turn, influenced a range of other coins from both England and the Continent attesting to its importance and, no doubt, the overall size of the issue (also see Finds 14 and 19).

Series A *sceat* from East Challow, Oxfordshire (BERK-220047).

The influence of Series A on other coins struck in England. Top: Series C (CAM-E7D4F4); bottom: Series R (FAJN-93ED7B).

The influence of Series A on continental *sceattas*. Top: Series D (LVPL-E6D101); bottom: Series E (BH-0A38B1).

**13. A silver *sceat* of Primary Phase Series B, *c.* 675–90, from Dymock, Gloucestershire (GLO-9BD812)**
Diameter: 12 mm; weight: 1.13 g.

The circulation of early medieval coins thinned towards the north and west of Britain, and this coin is one of relatively few *sceattas* found west of the River Severn. It is also a good example of the complex iconography on early pennies. The obverse follows Merovingian coinage with its clear diademed bust and inscription (although it is meaningless on these coins), while the reverse is innovative showing a bird on a cross. The bird probably represents the Holy Spirit, and its placement on a cross is a motif known in the early medieval Christian world from the eastern Mediterranean to northern Europe. The earliest type of Series B (BX) has the cross on a set of steps, ultimately copying Byzantine coinage (see Find 9). Both designs are enclosed in a pellet circle with a small 'v' shape at the bottom. This represents a snake biting its own tail, an ancient and well-known symbol of protection.

Series Bii *sceat* from Dymock, Gloucestershire (GLO-9BD812).

Series BX *sceat* (PUBLIC-BF2273).

**14. A Low Countries *sceat* of Series E, *c.* 700–720, from Cliffe and Cliffe Woods, Kent (SUR-5A8EE3)**
Diameter: 12.6 mm; weight: 1.18 g.

The most commonly found *sceattas* are those belonging to Series E, nicknamed 'porcupines' after their spiky obverse design. They account for around 20–30 per cent of all *sceattas* recorded by the PAS. In reality, Series E is a very diverse group produced over a period of perhaps sixty years. They were minted mostly in Frisia (Netherlands) and around the river delta formed by the Rhine, Meuse and Scheldt where two important early medieval ports, Domburg and Dorestad, were located. Found around the coastal strip of the North Sea, along rivers and land routes into both England and continental Europe, they epitomise the active networks of trade that flourished in the later seventh and eighth centuries. This coin was found near to the north Kent coast on the route towards London, an important port. This belongs to Series E's earliest phase, dating to around 700–20, the design within the box-shaped standard on the reverse possibly forming the letters V-I-C-O. It might relate to the Latin word *vicus*, often seen in the place names of ports and trading places at this time.

Series E *sceat* from Cliffe and Cliffe Woods, Kent (SUR-5A8EE3).

Examples of early issues of Series E *sceattas*. Top: plumed bird (LVPL-6F706D); bottom: Variety G (HAMP-674883).

Examples of later issues of Series E *sceattas*. Top: FAJN-93C008; bottom: SUR-53AB4D.

**15. A Secondary Phase *sceat* of Series H (type 39), *c.* 720–40, from Goodworth Clatford, Hampshire (HAMP-EF93DD)**
Diameter: 12 mm; weight 0.98 g.

The late seventh–eighth centuries witnessed the first town-like places in Britain since the Roman period. Located on rivers with easy access to the coast at London, Southampton, Ipswich and York, their populations were mostly involved in craft production and trade. Coins minted at these places form some of the larger groups, finds often concentrated in the regions around each port. Series H is made up from three related designs, their distribution clustering in the region behind the Solent. These were probably all struck in the port town of Hamwic (Southampton). The design has Christian iconography: a large Celtic cross with rosettes in-between the cross arms and in the centre on one side, and a bird in a vine – the pellets can be thought of as grapes – on the other. This common motif is seen in manuscripts, sculpture and art in this period, and may be a representation of heavenly paradise.

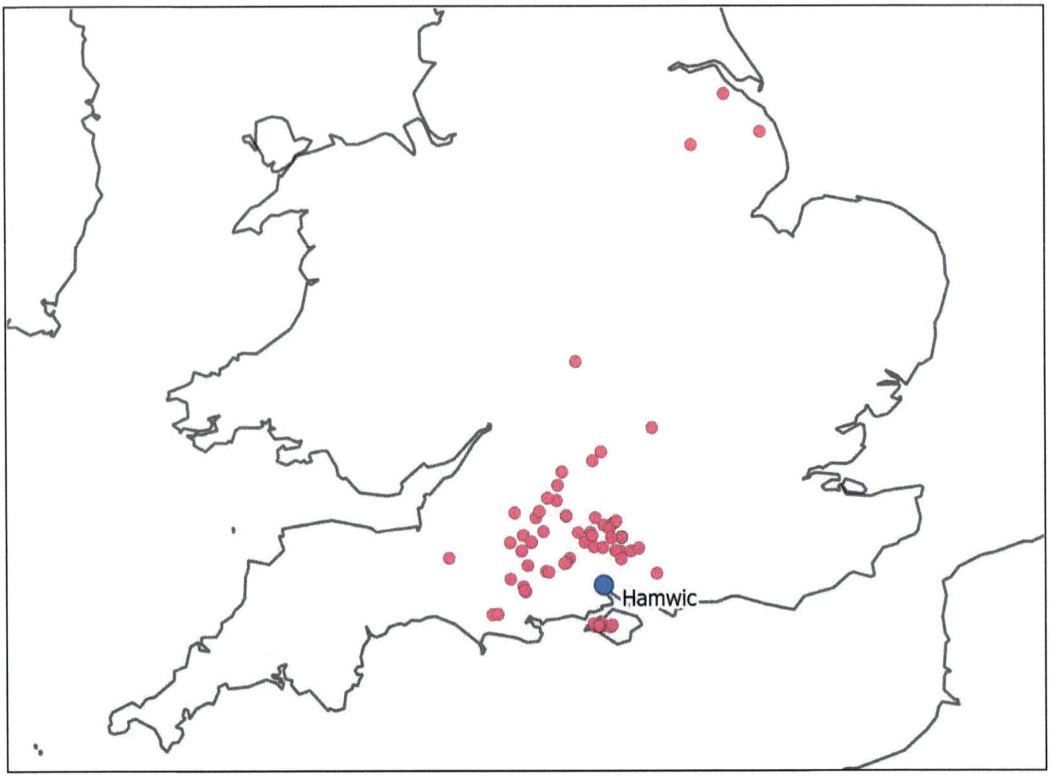


Map showing PAS-recorded finds of Series H and the location of Hamwic (Southampton), the likely mint place.

Series H (type 39) *sceat* from Goodworth Clatford, Hampshire (HAMP-EF93DD).

Series H (type 48; BERK-F3F6C8).

Series H (type 49; IOW-6F4D10).

**16. A Secondary Phase *sceat* of Series U, *c.* 710–25/30, from Woodham Mortimer, Essex (ESS-B3F243)**
Diameter: 11.8 mm; weight: 1.26 g.

The artistic style of Secondary Phase *sceattas* has long been admired, their designs often interpreted within the prism of Christian belief (also see Finds 13 and 15). A good example is the depiction of a standing figure, generally placed between crosses or a combination of cross and bird/plants. None of these types are found in large numbers and it is possible that at least some were issued by religious communities. Archaeological evidence has shown that many probable monastic sites were wealthy and well connected with regional, even international, contacts. This coin belongs to Series U and shows the standing figure with arms bent to hold a cross on either side. These crosses might be protective motifs and the figure stands in a crescent shape, probably representing a boat. Boats often served as a symbol for the Church providing safe passage. The figure itself is female, her identify uncertain but likely a saint or even Mary. The reverse shows a bird eating grapes from the vine, the same motif discussed in Find 15.

Series U *sceat* from Woodham Mortimer, Essex (ESS-B3F243).

The variety of *sceattas*. Top row: Series F (YORYM-9A778D); Series W (IOW-80D664). Row 2: Series G (LIN-D46FDB); Series K (BUC-C2FD5B). Row 3: Animal mask type (WILT-F7AA27); Series QII (LIN-7207F5). Row 4: Bust-with-cup type (IOW-8099B8); Sede type (DOR-AD9846). Bottom row: Series L-related (HAMP-BDE8F9); Series S (BH-299A82).

**17. A contemporary copy of Secondary Phase *sceat* of Series J, *c.* 710–25, from Clothall, Bedfordshire (BH-019283)**
Diameter: 11.2 mm; weight: 0.7 g.

Counterfeiting coins is almost as old as coinage itself. This coin is an early medieval example of such a practice, the design now hard to see because of corrosion. Rather than being made from silver its core is copper alloy with a thin coating of silver on top to make it look genuine. The design copies coins of Series J (type 36), a common issue with widespread distribution originating in the Humber region. This example cannot be considered an official issue, the silver coating suggesting it was made to deceive. Counterfeits tend to be known for the major types, with examples of the 'porcupines' of Series E also known to be struck on copper-alloy flans.

Contemporary copy of a Series J (type 36) *sceat* from Clothall, Bedfordshire (BH-019283).

A regular silver issue of a Series J (type 36) *sceat* (YORYM-2DA228).

**18. A Danish *sceat* of Series X, *c.* 720–60, from Redlynch, Wiltshire (FAJN-1C0291)**
Diameter: 11.5 mm; weight: 1.08 g.

The coins of Series X originated in the town of Ribe (Denmark), an important port like Ipswich and Southampton. First produced around 720, excavations in the town showed that they were used throughout the eighth century. They have a slightly odd distribution in Britain, with clusters in the Wessex heartlands from southern Oxfordshire to the Solent, and from Lincolnshire to East Yorkshire, but very few East Anglian finds have been recorded. This coin is in good condition, a wild-haired, bearded face with crosses either side on the obverse, and a backwards-looking animal on the reverse, which is a common motif in early medieval art. The bust is often referred to as 'Wodan' but in reality the style is based on regional art traditions and such a face is seen on some earlier coins. Imitations of Series X were produced in England too, including some in which the animal on the reverse is rendered more in a style akin to other Secondary Phase *sceattas*. That these Danish coins found their way to Britain in large numbers, along with other Continental coins (see Find 14), is testament to the levels of trade occurring around the southern parts of the North Sea coasts. This brought in goods and raw materials from further afield, too, some of it high status items such as wines and spices, and some more utilitarian such as lava quernstones from Germany used for grinding grain which are found across eastern England.

Series X *sceat* from Redlynch, Wiltshire (FAJN-1C0291).

Traditions in early medieval art styles and Series X coins. Top: Series Z (YORYM-1FA305); bottom: Series N, type 41b (BERK-D47F3D).

Top: Series X local imitation (IOW-0372B7); bottom: Series O, type 40 (SF-9C9E51).

Ninth-century strap end with Trewhiddle-style backwards-looking animal decoration (WMID-4462B7).

**19. A Secondary Phase *sceat* of Series R, *c.* 730–50, from Caistor St Edmund, Norfolk (NMS-2DB7E8)**
Diameter: 12 mm; weight: 0.83 g.

Unlike the counterfeit coin (Find 17) the patches of green copper corrosion on this one are not due to counterfeiting but to low silver content, which is typical of the later *sceattas*. By the 740s the silver content in these coins had declined to under 50 per cent with more copper mixed into the alloy, and this can be seen clearly on the surface. It belongs at the end of a large East Anglian group, Series R, probably struck primarily at Ipswich and found across the region. The design can be traced back to the Primary Phase coins of Series A (Find 12) but the bust is now more abstract with a very prominent mouth, nose and eye; there is no discernible neck. The runic inscription spells a name, most likely that of a moneyer, *wigrœd*. Stray finds of this late type are rare, this one of just three recorded by the PAS. The maps show the distribution of finds is focused in the eastern half of England, most densely in southern East Anglia. Other finds illustrate both coastal and inland contacts, those heading inland using the ancient routes of the Icknield Way towards to the Thames Valley and beyond, no doubt representing trade in both directions.

Series R (type R10) *sceat* from Caistor St Edmund, Norfolk (NMS-2DB7E8).

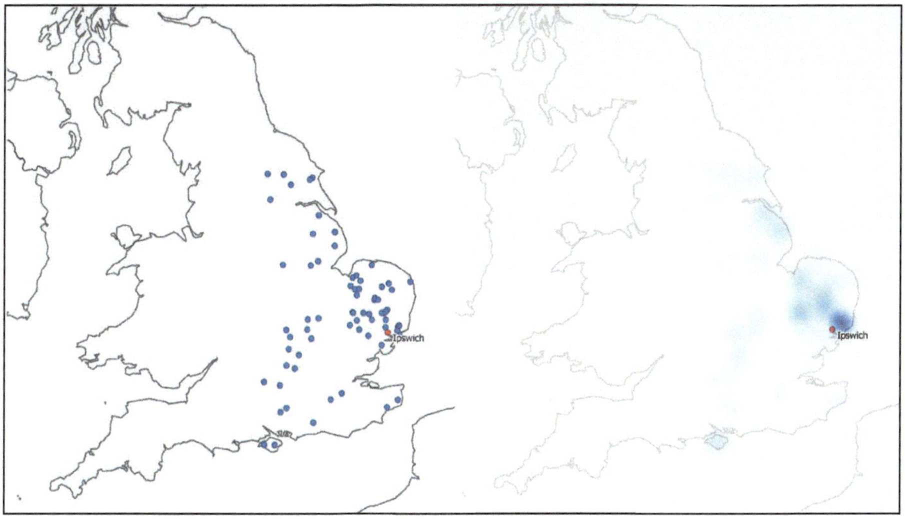


The distribution of PAS-recorded *sceattas* of Series R (left) and a 'heat map' showing the density of these finds (right).

Some types of Series R showing variations in bust styles and reverse types. Top: Series R2 (BH-4B9CD3); bottom: Series R3 (IOW-41F4B8).

Top: Series R8 (LIN-D62F8C); bottom: Series R3 var (BUC-73B11A).

**20. Penny of Eadberht of Northumbria, *c.* 737–58, from Kilham, East Yorkshire (FAKL-37C614)**
Diameter: 14.4 mm; weight: 0.9 g.

Northumbrian coinage continued to use small, thick flans into the ninth century, but from the issues of Eadberht (757–58) onwards they were an explicitly royal coinage with the king's name on the coin. The design references the issues of Aldfrith of Northumbria (685–704), which also named the king and placed a four-legged beast with a long tail, defined snout and raised front leg on the reverse. The design lasted until the reign of Ælfwald I (778/9–88). The animal might be a representation of a lion, and similar creatures are seen elsewhere in early medieval art. The distribution of these Northumbrian coins is also informative. Concentrated north of the Humber, especially on the Yorkshire Wolds, they are much more common than contemporary non-local issues which must have been excluded from the circulating currency and reminted. Such control over the currency was not seen elsewhere for some time. It is likely that there was a mint at York – Northumbrian kings sometimes jointly issued coins with the archbishops there (see Find 26) – where the Church had a central position and archaeology shows us that the city had wide contacts across Britain and abroad. Other mint places are likely, too, probably at rural royal estates.

Penny of Eadberht from Kilham, East Yorkshire (FAKL-37C614).

Penny of Aldfrith, 685–704 (NMS-576BB5).

Penny of Alchred, 765–74 (YORYM-D21472).

**21. Penny of Offa of Mercia, *c.* 765–92, from Shottesbrooke, Windsor & Maidenhead (SUR-9A3435)**
Diameter: 16.7 mm; weight: 1.21 g.

A profound change in the coinage came during the reign of Offa (757–96), whose Mercian kingdom controlled much of southern England. He introduced silver pennies struck on broader, thinner flans, the coins now naming the king, here OFFA REX (King Offa). Another innovation was the inclusion of the name of the moneyer, in this case Pendred, who struck coins in London. There were only two other mints, Canterbury, the country's most important, and one in East Anglia, probably at Ipswich. Produced in better quality silver than the final *sceattas*, they are found in lower numbers and their distribution is less widespread. This coin is a good example of the artistic quality of Offa's coinage and the influence from Roman coinage. Offa is shown in profile, wearing armour in a way typically seen on fourth-century Imperial coins. Above his head, though, is a coiled snake, a motif seen in early medieval art and interpreted as a symbol of protection.

Penny of Offa from Shottesbrooke, Windsor & Maidenhead (SUR-9A3435).

The art of Offa's coinage. Top row: BUC-D5B3E5; LEIC-94EB56. Row 2: SF-05E1F4; OXON-68253D. Row 3: KENT-2844F3; IOW-C8BD83. Bottom row: LIN-51BE26; LIN-17B266.

**22. Penny of Cynethryth of Mercia, *c.* 765–92, from the Aiskew hoard, North Yorkshire (YORYM-731473)**
Diameter: 16.7 mm; weight: 1.31 g.

Cynethryth was the wife of Offa of Mercia and our evidence suggests she played an important role in his court and the broader kingdom, witnessing charters as the 'Queen of the Mercians'. She is also the only early medieval woman to have coins struck in her name, even if others such as Æthelflaed, the 'Lady of the Mercians', are more famous. Cynethryth's portrait issue was influenced by Roman coins, especially those of Faustina I, who was the wife of Antoninus Pius (138–61). Cynethryth's coins have similar style in the hair, face and drapery. Two types were struck for her at Canterbury by the moneyer Eoba from around 784–92 and the numbers of finds suggest that they were struck in quite large numbers. This coin was found as part of a small hoard of coins, a rare find from Offa's reign. An important coin found recently is a new type for Cynethryth struck at the mint in London rather than at Canterbury. Although it is damaged, the coin's inscription tells us it was struck by the moneyer Ludomon who also produced coins for Offa in the city.

Penny of Cynethryth from Aiskew, North Yorkshire (YORYM-731473).

Non-portrait type pennies of Cynethryth. Top: minted at Canterbury by Eoba (HAMP-73ADA0). Bottom: minted at London by Ludomon (SF-7B972E).

Roman *denarius* of Faustina I (ASHM-B1D41D).

**23. Penny of Eadberht III 'Præn' of Kent, 796–8, from Tiverton, Cheshire (LVPL-C15BC5)**
Diameter: 19 mm; weight: 1.2 g.

In 796, Offa died and his son Ecgfrith became king of the Mercians. He died later the same year to be replaced by a distant cousin, Coenwulf (796–821). The kingdoms of East Anglia and Kent took advantage of the crisis to reclaim independence, and coins were struck for their rulers. Finds are very rare, and this is only the second coin recorded by the PAS for Eadberht III 'Præn' of Kent (796–8). It was minted at Canterbury by the moneyer Æthelnoth, who had also produced coins for Offa, its design copying Coenwulf's 'tribrach' coinage from London. Coenwulf soon retook control, taking Eadberht to Mercia, blinded and maimed, and installed his own brother, Cuthred (798–807), as sub-king of Kent.

Penny of Eadberht III 'Præn' from Tiverton, Cheshire (LVPL-C15BC5).

Penny of Coenwulf's 'tribrach' type minted in London, which influenced the issues Eadberht III 'Præn' (SUR-F72DA7).

Penny of Cuthred, sub-king of Kent (BH-5B5B60).

Coinage of independent Kent. Top: anonymous Kent issue, 822–3 (LANCUM-B35275); bottom: Baldred, sub-king of Kent, 823–5 (SUR-1FBC42).

## 24. Penny of Coenwulf of Mercia, *c.* 800–21, from Boxgrove, West Sussex (HAMP-BD4675)

Alongside the important mints in Kent and London, Mercian coins were also struck in East Anglia, most likely at Ipswich. This coin is typical of Coenwulf's East Anglian issues with a bust on the obverse and cross motif on the reverse. It has been suggested that this design influenced those produced later at Canterbury, the country's most important mint. Coins struck in East Anglia for Coenwulf are not common finds, but the dozen recorded by the PAS have a coastal distribution outside of the immediate mint region with one from Lincolnshire and a number, including this one, along the south coast. This suggests that they were dispersed via maritime routes. The designs seen on Coenwulf's coinage are not as diverse as those under Offa suggesting that there was control over the images and motifs used, with the artistic freedom available to those cutting the dies more restricted. Like on Offa's coins, the bust is still based on Roman coins, although this is not always well produced, and it has been suggested that rather than just imitation it had become an idealised way to represent the king.

Penny of Coenwulf from Boxgrove, West Sussex (HAMP-BD4675).

Examples of Coenwulf pennies recorded by the PAS. Top: large portrait type, moneyer: Wærheard, mint: Canterbury (WMID-E12467); bottom: large portrait/cross-and-crosslets type, moneyer: Aelfhun, mint: London (WILT-CDE44E).

Top: cross-and-wedges type, moneyer: Eoba, mint: Canterbury (SWYOR-0B56E5); bottom: portrait type, moneyer: Lul, mint: Ipswich (NMS-30AA8C).

**25. *Styca* of Eanred of Northumbria, *c.* 810–41, from Skirpenbeck, East Riding of Yorkshire (YORYM-D3453A)**
Diameter: 13.3 mm; weight: 1 g.

During the reign of Ælfwald I (779/80–89) the Northumbrian 'fantastic beast' design (Find 20) was replaced by a simple central motif, often a roundel or cross, around which was the king's name (obverse) and the moneyer (reverse). Still struck on small, thick flans, they remained very different to the issues of the southern kingdoms of Mercia, Wessex and East Anglia. Known as *stycas* (a term from documentary evidence wrongly attributed to them in the seventeenth century), their silver content declined rapidly in the early ninth century, becoming a low-value copper-alloy coin unique in northern Europe. The PAS has recorded more than 500 and some very large hoards are known, such as one from Hexham containing over 8,000 coins. The bulk of these finds come from east of the Pennines from the River Tees to the Lincolnshire fenland near the Wash, and a few others in East Anglia and Upper Thames Valley. This coin of Eanred (810–40) was struck by the moneyer Eadwine and remains in good condition, the increasing amount of copper in the alloy visible as green corrosion on its surface.

*Styca* of Eanred from Skirpenbeck, East Riding of Yorkshire (YORYM-D3453A).

Northumbrian *stycas* struck for other rulers. Top: Æthelred I's 2nd reign, 790–6, moneyer Ceolbald (FAKL-DD7752); Ælfwald II, 806–808, moneyer Cuthheard (YORYM-BAECA8). Row 2: Æthelred II's 1st reign, 840/1–4, moneyer Ealhhere (FAKL-EE8913); Redwulf, 844–?, moneyer Fordred (FAKL-86B186). Row 3: Æthelred II's 2nd reign, 844–8?, moneyer Eardwulf (YORYM-889249); Osberht, 848/9–62/3, moneyer Wynebeorht (DENO-03ACC2). Row 4: late blundered *styca* (YORYM-69D86B); weight with *styca*, probably of Redwulf, embedded in top (NMS-0D47D0).

**26. Penny of Archbishop Wulfred of Canterbury, *c.* 815–22, from Lighthorne, Warwickshire (WAW-238254)**
Weight: 1.3 g.

Kings were not alone in issuing coins between the eighth and early tenth centuries with the Archbishops of Canterbury and York also doing so, sometimes jointly with the king. The silver pennies from Canterbury are not common finds – only one or two are recorded by the PAS each year – but they circulated widely. This coin of Archbishop Wulfred of Canterbury (805–32) dates to *c.* 815–22 when Kent was still under Mercian control, and it was found in the Mercian heartlands. Wulfred's coins are the first ecclesiastical issues to have a portrait, clearly showing his tonsured head and copying late eighth-century coins of the Pope of Rome. The reverse of this coin gives the moneyer's name, Saeberht, and in the centre is a monogram of *Dorovernia* (the ancient name for Canterbury), a style influenced by issues of the Carolingian Emperor Charlemagne.

Penny of Archbishop Wulfred from Lighthorne, Warwickshire (WAW-238254).

Early medieval pennies of the Archbishops of Canterbury and York, their rarity obvious from the condition of some of these examples. Top row (Canterbury): Archbishop Jaenberht with Offa of Mercia (LIN-6DA4A4); Archbishop Æthelheard with Coenwulf of Mercia (GLO-7FA598). Row 2 (Canterbury): Archbishop Ceolnoth (centre of coin only; LEIC-D7641E); Archbishop Æthelred (SUR-4A4231). Row 3: Archbishop Plegmund of Canterbury (OXON-B49585); Archbishop Ecgberht of York with Æthelwold Moll (YORYM-9F55B2). Bottom row (York): Archbishop Eanbald II (YORYM-0338A8); Archbishop Wigmund (YORYM-6D2CAD); Archbishop Wulfhere of York (NLM-09595). Images of Archbishop Æthelred of Canterbury (SUR-4A4231) are © Ashmolean Museum, University of Oxford.

**27. Penny of Ecgberht of Wessex, *c.* 828–39, from Watlington, Oxfordshire (BH-3E6308)**
Diameter: 20.7 mm; weight: 1.3 g.

Coenwulf's death in 821 resulted in a number of short-lived successors to the Mercian throne, accompanied by a loss of power and territory that ended the century-long overlordship the kingdom had enjoyed over most of southern England. Wessex reasserted itself and in 825 defeated Mercian forces at the Battle of Wroughton. Ecgberht took control of Kent and its important mints at Canterbury and Rochester, vital additions to the small mint in Wessex, probably located at Winchester or Southampton. Finds are rare and this coin was struck in Canterbury by the moneyer Swefheard, its design including the *Dorovernia* monogram (Find 26). The broad distribution of Ecgberht's coinage is densest in Wessex, its new lands in the south-east and some from East Anglia; few finds come from Mercia.

Penny of Ecgberht from Watlington, Oxfordshire (BH-3E6308).

Pennies of Ecgberht from (top) the mint in Wessex (IOW-05DF24) and (bottom) in Rochester (WAW-A3B0D2).

*Above left*: Coinage of Coenwulf of Mercia's short-lived successors (top to bottom): Ceolwulf I, 821–3 (SF-E287C0); Beornwulf, 823–5 (BUC-C35E01); Ludica, 825–7 (WMID-7A2DC2).

*Above right*: Examples of typical eighth and ninth-century object types: pin (BUC-DADAE8), strap end (BERK-04A9D4).

Hooked tag (left; OXON-6480CB); strip brooch (right; WILT-BF6D98).

**28. Penny of Æthelstan I of East Anglia, *c.* 825–45, from Llantwit Major, Vale of Glamorgan (NMGW-DAB2C6)**
Weight: 1.27 g.

East Anglian independence from Mercia occurred sometime during the reign of the Mercian king Ludica (825–7). The situation is so poorly understood that the East Anglian ruler Æthelstan I is known only from his coinage, the approximate dates of his reign *c.* 825–45. This shows that neither Mercia or Wessex asserted control over the region until Wessex's conquests of the tenth century. Æthelstan I's coinage is divided between early types with portraits, like this one, and later non-portrait types. The design on this coin is very similar in style to those struck by the Mercian kings Ceolwulf I (821–3) and Beornwulf (823–5) including in their East Anglian issues. It was struck by the moneyer Mon, the reverse inscription reading MON MONETA in three lines, although the second line, MONE, is upside down. The PAS has recorded twenty-five to date, their distribution focused towards eastern regions including along the coasts north and south. This coin is the most westerly discovery, and one of few early medieval coins from Wales.

Penny of Æthelstan I from Llantwit Major, Vale of Glamorgan (NMGW-DAB2C6).

Coinage of the East Anglian kings: Æthelweard, *c.* 845–55 (SF-793F43); Edmund, 855–69 (SF-E1C3B5).

**29. Penny of Burgred of Mercia, *c.* 865–8, from Adisham, Kent (KENT-4FC763)**
Diameter: 19.5 mm; weight: 1.18 g.

Although diminished by the expansion of Wessex and loss of East Anglia, Mercia remained an important kingdom. Alliances were built up with Wessex through marriage and military co-operation, and economic ties are visible in the coinage. The two kingdoms issued the same types of coins, known as 'lunettes' after the shapes above and below the moneyer's name on the reverse. Two kings of Wessex, Æthelred I (865–71) and Alfred (871–99), adopted this design, which was introduced by Burgred in the early years of his reign. This penny of Burgred of Mercia (852–74) was struck in London by the moneyer Cenred, the style of the bust and shape of the lunettes placing production in the late 860s, during the period of joint issue with Wessex. Known mostly from hoards, the PAS has recorded fewer than thirty lunettes pennies in total, most of them in the name of Burgred. It is likely that the coins of each kingdom were mostly struck at different mints, in general the Mercian coins at London and Wessex coins at Canterbury. Alfred probably continued to strike lunettes pennies after Burgred abdicated in 874 and by this time they were struck from poor quality silver with a reform of the coinage and raising of the silver content happening soon afterwards.

Penny of Burgred from Adisham, Kent (KENT-4FC763).

Lunettes pennies in the name of Æthelred I of Wessex (top; KENT-AE7FE8) and Alfred of Wessex (bottom; PUBLIC-A00281).

A hoard of stacked-up, fused lunettes pennies (WAW-8ED697).

**30. Silver pennies of Alfred of Wessex and Ceolwulf II of Mercia, *c.* 875–79, from the 'Watlington area' hoard, Oxfordshire (SUR-4A4231)**
Alfred: diameter: 19.9 mm; weight: 1.42 g.
Ceolwulf: diameter: 20 mm; weight: 1.23 g.

In 874, Mercia was defeated by the Vikings and Burgred exiled, bringing Ceolwulf II (874–*c.* 879) to the Mercian throne. Described in the *Anglo-Saxon Chronicle* as 'a foolish king's thegn' and puppet of the Vikings, historians now consider his position as Mercian king more favourably. Part of this rehabilitation is due to the coinage issued during his reign, which saw Wessex and Mercia continuing production of pennies using the same designs. These two coins come from the Watlington Hoard, which contains around 200 coins (and other precious metal objects). Both belong to the Cross-and-Lozenge coinage that was struck at several mints, probably London, Canterbury, Winchester and at least one other location, possibly in West Mercia. Both coins were struck in the 'London style' by the prolific moneyer Liafwald, spelt Liofwald on most of Ceolwulf's coins, in much better silver than the final lunettes pennies of Burgred and Alfred, showing that they were a serious attempt at coin reform. They also illustrate the continuing alliance between the two kingdoms even if the history written a little later in Wessex tried to paint a different picture. The Watlington Hoard is one of the most important late ninth-century hoards ever found. Most of the coins are extremely rare types, the majority being of the Cross-and-Lozenge type along with 13 examples of the Two Emperors type which was based on the Roman *solidus* seen in Find 10. It is possible that the two seated figures on this coin type represent an alliance between the Alfred and Ceolwulf II, Wessex and Mercia being the only two kingdoms not wholly defeated by the Vikings. The hoard was buried near Watlington around 879–80 which is an area through which the Icknield Way passes on its route to East Anglia. Alfred's forces had beaten the Vikings at the Battle of Edington in Wiltshire in 878, their leader Guthrum accepting Christianity and, after spending the winter at Cirencester in Gloucestershire, the army had left for East Anglia to settle. The easiest route for them to have taken was via the Icknield Way and so it is possible that the burial of this collection of coins, Scandinavian jewellery and ingots was connected to this event, possibly even buried by a Viking from the 'Great Army'.

'Cross-and-Lozenge' type pennies of Alfred and Ceolwulf II from the 'Watlington area' hoard, Oxfordshire (SUR-4A4231) © Ashmolean Museum, University of Oxford.

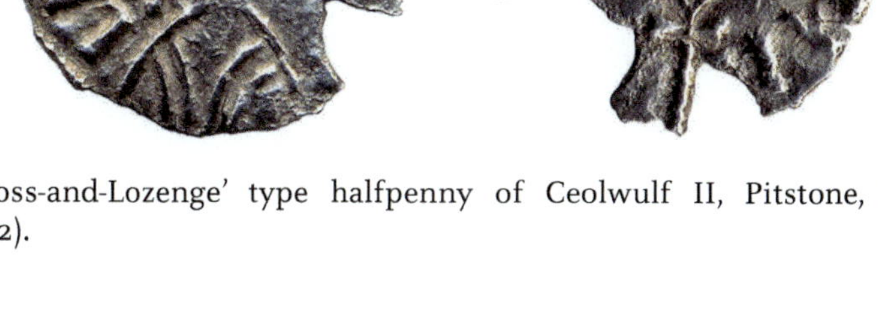

Unique 'Cross-and-Lozenge' type halfpenny of Ceolwulf II, Pitstone, Buckinghamshire (BUC-08EE42).

**31. Imitation of a Carolingian gold *solidus*, ninth century, from near Eye, Suffolk (SF-5DE284)**
Diameter: 19.8 mm; weight: 4.03 g.

Gold coins became very rare after the late seventh century and were not regularly struck again until the mid-fourteenth century. A handful of eighth- and ninth-century gold issues struck for the kings of Mercia are known, each one unique, but the biggest group are those imitating *solidi* struck for the Carolingian ruler Louis the Pious (814–40). Found quite widely in eastern England and along the south coast, as well as in the Low Countries, it appears that they originate from either England or the Netherlands. The obverse on this coin has a right-facing bust, while the reverse has a simple cross within a beaded circle. The inscriptions are garbled versions of the original. It is hard to know how these coins were used given their rarity – the PAS has recorded five examples compared to over 400 eighth–ninth-century pennies – but it is likely that such high-value coins would have had a role in long-distance commerce, land purchase and as a store of bullion.

Imitation of a Carolingian gold *solidus* from near Eye, Suffolk (SF-5DE284).

Carolingian *denier* from Grade-Ruan, Cornwall (CORN-079B27).

**32. Silver Carolingian *denier*, ninth century, from Grade-Ruan, Cornwall (CORN-079B27)**
Diameter: 20 mm; weight: 1.45 g.

At its height the empire of the Carolingians stretched across much of what is now France, Germany and the Low Countries and into Spain and Italy. Its coinage is only found rarely in Britain, probably reminted into local currency when it entered the country. Finds are widely distributed and have been made at ports such as Southampton and Ipswich. It is likely that at least some relate to Viking activity as they are a common element in Viking hoards from the late ninth and tenth centuries. This silver *denier*, a very rare find of an early medieval coin from Cornwall, belongs to a type known as a 'Karolus monogram' type – the name referring to the monogram of letters in the centre of the reverse – which was minted at Melle (France), where important silver mines were in operation. The 'Karolus Monogram' was minted during Charlemagne's reign (768–814) and from Charles the Bald (844–70) into the tenth century. The similar styles make dating difficult but this one probably belongs to either Charlemagne or Charles the Bald rather than a tenth-century variety. The rarity of Continental coinage in Britain belies the Carolingian influence on art and material culture, which can be seen across a broad range of objects.

Silver *denier* of Louis the Pious, Christiana Religio type (LIN-F6C6E1).

Examples of PAS-recorded Carolingian objects: silver gilt strap end (NMS-55FBD7); copper-alloy trefoil mount (LEIC-C5F14A); silver gilt harness fitting (KENT-02AD2D).

# Chapter 3
# From the Viking Age to the Norman Conquest: *c.* 880–1066

During the 880s, Alfred the Great and the Vikings agreed to a division of England into a Wessex-dominated area in the west and south, and the 'Danelaw' in the east and north where a number of Viking rulers held sway. The conquest of the Danelaw, mostly by Edward the Elder (899–924) with his sister Æthelflæd 'Lady of the Mercians' and Athelstan (924–39), brought England under a single king. Many of the spectacular Viking hoards found in northern England were buried in this period. The Viking legacy is also seen in many Scandinavian place names in the Danelaw that survive to this day, and tenth- and eleventh-century art styles emerged with a hybrid 'Anglo-Scandinavian' style. The wealth of the state and aristocracy increased from the later tenth century as the countryside was reorganised and towns became vital central places, developing out of the fortified settlements, or *burhs*, founded as defence against the Vikings. The currency, too, became more stable and progressively more important. The renewal of Viking activity, especially in the early eleventh century, resulted in enormous tributes being paid and there are large hoards of English coinage known from Scandinavia. The culmination of this was the long and successful reign of the Danish king Cnut (1016–42). The problems of succession following Edward the Confessor's death in 1066 brought even more profound change with the accession of the Norman rulers under William the Conqueror.

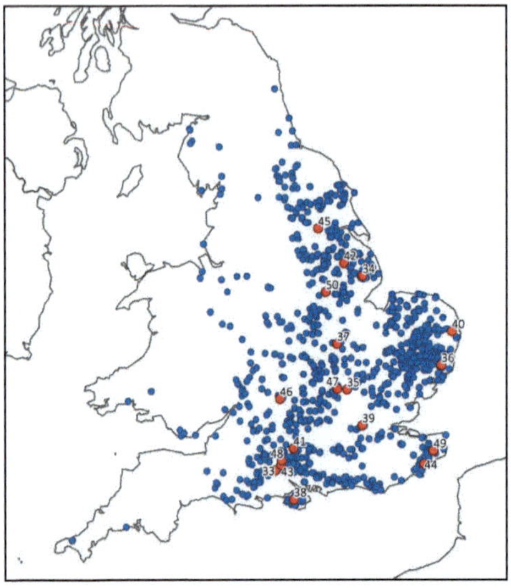

Map of PAS-recorded coin finds dating *c.* 880–*c.* 973 and showing the location of Finds 33–50.

**33. Penny of Alfred, *c.* 879/80–99, from the Salisbury area, Wiltshire (WILT-7B3827)**
Diameter: 20 mm; weight: 1.51 g.

Around 879/80 another change in coin design occurred introducing a style that lasted into the reign of Edgar (959–75). This new design simply states the king's name around a central cross on the obverse and the moneyer's name placed horizontally in two lines on the reverse – hence the 'Horizontal/Two-Line' type – with other motifs between, above and below. This coin shows Alfred's name in three sections, ÆLF RE DRE (spelling ÆLFRED RE, King Alfred), and the moneyer is named as Wulfred (VVLF/RED on the coin). The three-way division of the obverse inscription has been attributed to coins from Winchester, with Wulfred a known Winchester moneyer from the Cross-and-Lozenge coinage. Two-line coins were regularly copied by the Vikings of the Danelaw but this one is heavy enough that it can be considered an official issue. Stray finds of two-line pennies of Alfred are rare.

Penny of Alfred from the Salisbury area, Wiltshire (WILT-7B3827).

Tenth-century 'Horizontal/Two-Line' types: Edward the Elder, 899–924 (NARC-39B244); Athelstan, 924–39 (IOW-BE51A4); Edmund, 939–46 (GLO-D7E0AE); Eadred, 946–55 (LANCUM-411E05); Eadwig, 955–9 (LANCUM-2AA274); Edgar, 959–75 (NLM-F2F19C).

**34. Penny of Cnut of Northumbria, *c.* 895–910, from Rearsby, Leicestershire (LEIC-B230B8)**
Diameter: 20 mm; weight: 1.28 g.

By the late ninth century Viking rulers in the Danelaw were beginning to produce their own coins and this one belongs to those struck in northern England from around 895–905/10. It is one of very few stray finds of its type, issued in the name of someone called Cnut – not to be confused with the later King Cnut (1016–35) – and was probably struck at York. Their designs are interesting, especially the use of Christian images. The reverse shows a patriarchal cross, which has an additional set of horizontal arms, copied from ninth-century Byzantine gold *solidi* of Theophilus I (829–42). Around this the letters spelling CNVT REX (where the V is read as U) seem randomly placed, but the letters C-N-V-T need to be read as if making the sign of the cross (top, bottom, left, right). This spells the ruler's name and extolls his Christian identity, placing these Viking rulers alongside Europe's Christian kings.

Penny of Cnut of Northumbria from Rearsby, Leicestershire (LEIC-B230B8).

Penny of another Danelaw ruler, Regnald I of York, *c.* 919–21 (NLM-F304C3).

**35. Penny in the name of St Edmund the Martyr, *c.* 895–915, from Offley, Hertfordshire (SUR-5F6EA5)**
Diameter: 18.6 mm; weight: 1.4 g

In 869 the Viking 'Great Army' invaded and conquered East Anglia, killing its king, Edmund (855–69). He was soon venerated as a saint and East Anglia's Viking rulers issued anonymous coins in his name from the mid-890s–*c.* 915. These are based on one of Edmund's own issues (see Find 28). The prefix SC was added to Edmund's name to denote his new saintly status. They are the most numerous Viking type on the PAS database with around forty recorded. Circulation was limited, tightly clustered in Norfolk, Suffolk and Cambridgeshire, this one coming from near the edge of the general distribution. It can be placed late in the sequence of issues from its rather garbled inscription, its obverse reading SCEAIDM rather than SC EADMVND R as seen in the early phases.

'St Edmund memorial type' penny from Offley, Hertfordshire (SUR-5F6EA5).

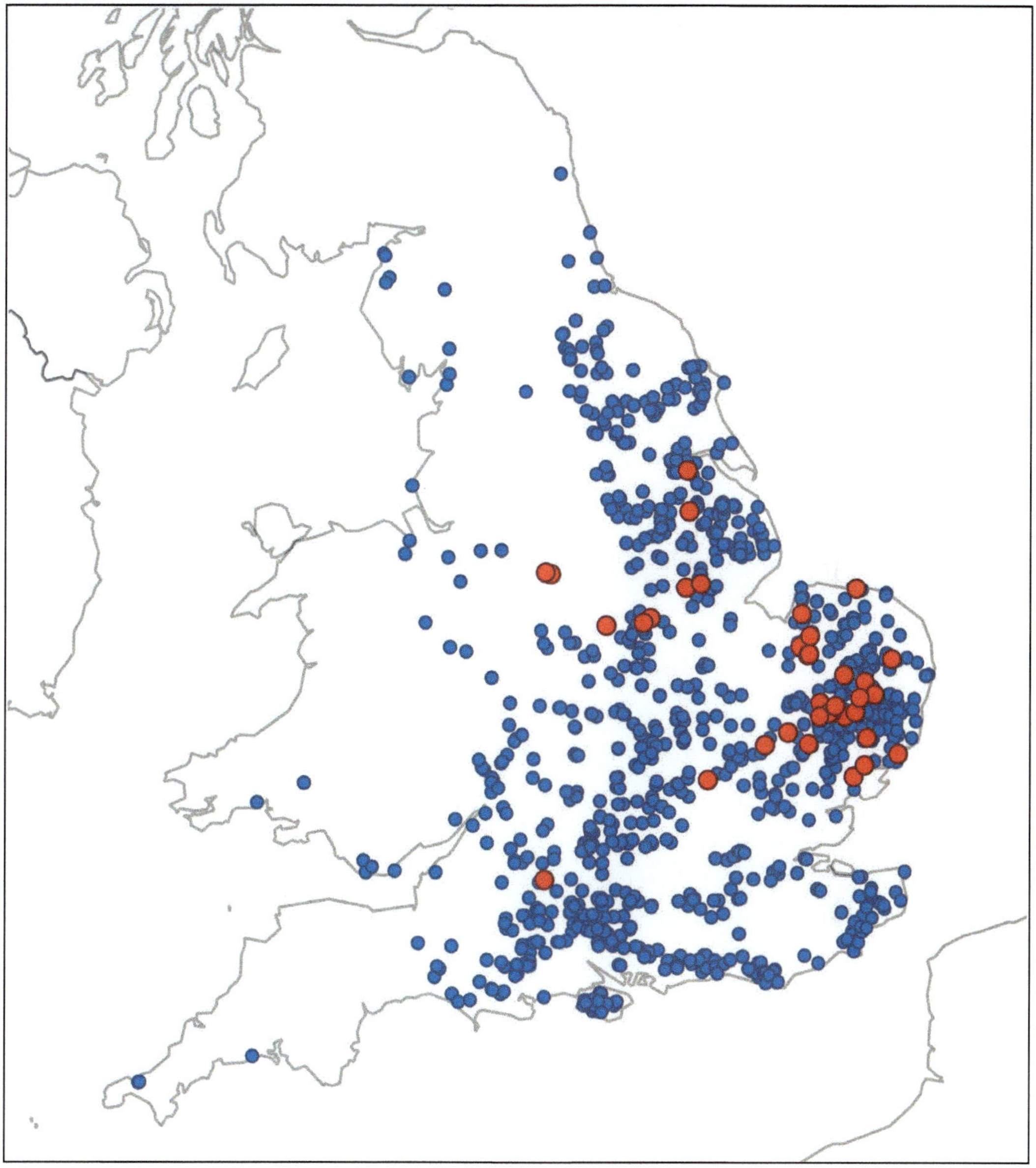

Map showing the distribution of PAS-recorded finds of St Edmund Memorial pennies (red dots) against the distribution of coin finds *c.* 880–1066 (blue dots).

**36. Penny of Swordless St Peter type, *c.* 910–19, from Campsey Ash, Suffolk (SF-735C71)**
Diameter:18.5 mm; weight: 1.15 g.

The Viking rulers of York also struck anonymous coins in the name of a saint, this time St Peter to whom York Minster was dedicated. The St Peter series, dating from *c.* 905–27, can be divided into two groups: an earlier 'swordless' type and a later one incorporating a sword into its design. None are common finds, especially outside of hoards. This coin belongs towards the end of the 'swordless' phase. We know this because the inscriptions are less literate versions of the original SCI PETRI MO (literally St Peter's money) on the obverse and EBORACE CIV (City of York) on the reverse, instead reading SCIIE/TRIII/CI and BCRACE. The use of the 'Horizontal/Two-Line' inscription style shows the influence of the Wessex coinage of Alfred and Edward the Elder on these coins. Like the other Viking issues (Finds 34–5), this coin shows Vikings consciously promoting their Christianity.

St Peter of York penny from Campsey Ash, Suffolk (SF-735C71).

St Peter of York 'sword' type penny dating to the 920s (DENO-FCA770).

**37. Islamic silver dirham, AH163/AD780, from the Aldwincle area, Northamptonshire (DENO-07CCA4)**
Diameter: 23.6 mm; weight: 2.54 g.

In the ninth and tenth centuries enormous amounts of coinage struck in the Middle East and Central Asia entered Europe, illustrating the long-distance trade routes in existence at the time. These coins are mostly silver dirhams, and are particularly common in hoards found in Scandinavia and Central/Eastern Europe. Smaller amounts are known in Britain and Ireland from areas associated with Viking activity and settlement, most cut up into pieces of hacksilver used in a bullion-based economy. Occasionally complete coins like this one are also found. Struck in Baghdad (Iraq) during the reign of the Abbasid Caliph Al-Mahdi Billah in AH163 (AD780), it is unlikely that the coin reached England until the late ninth or early tenth century. The Arabic inscriptions provide administrative information on the mint and issuer alongside long-standing religious quotations.

Islamic dirham from the Aldwincle area, Northamptonshire (DENO-07CCA4).

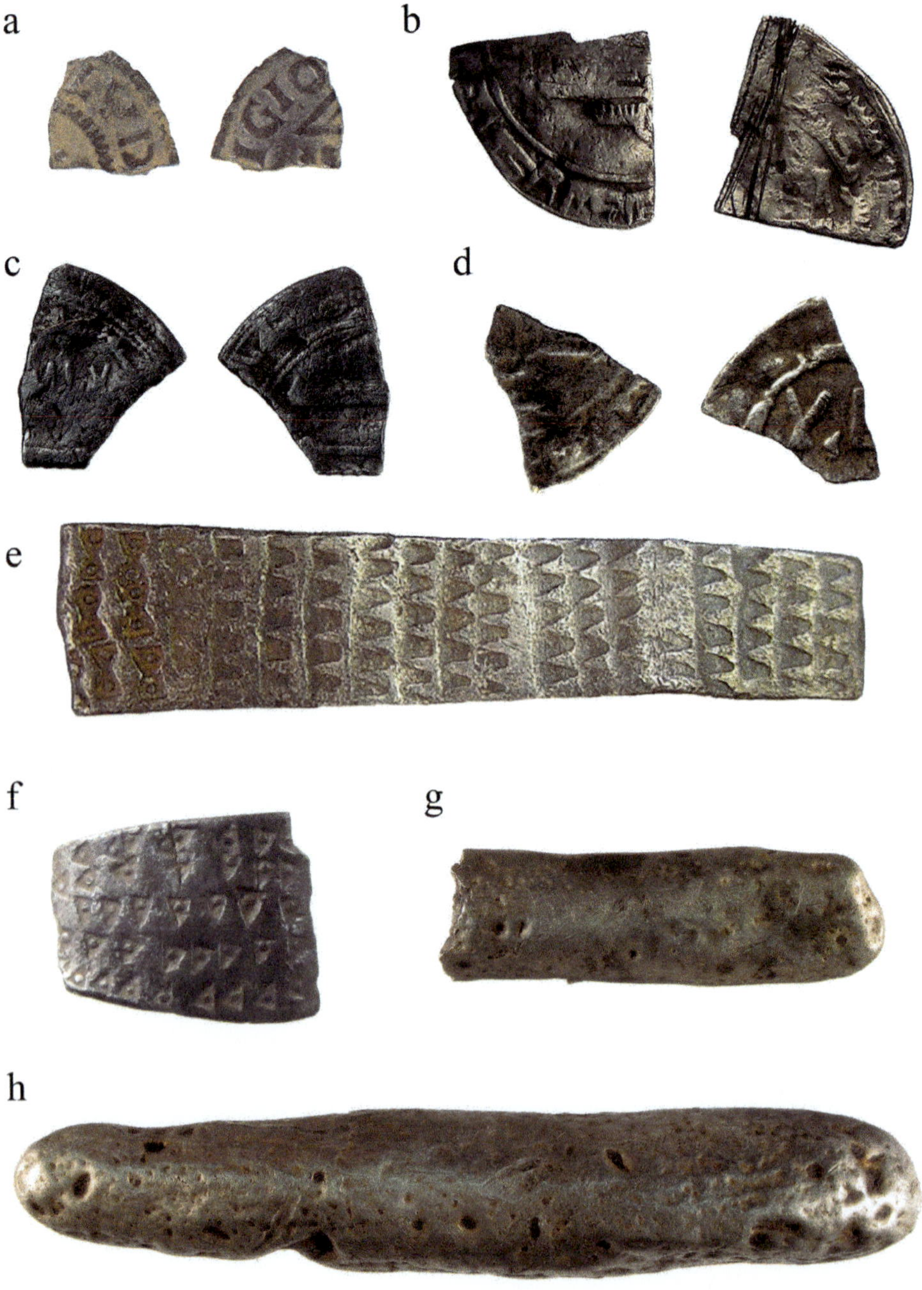


Hacksilver and ingots as evidence for a bullion economy. Hacksilver coins: (a) cut fragment of Carolingian *denier* from Skirpenbeck, East Riding of Yorkshire (YORYM-81FB8D); (b) cut fragment of Islamic dirham with cut marks on surface from Maltby, Rotherham (FAKL-984168); (c) and (d) cut fragments of Islamic dirham from Brampton, Lincolnshire (SWYOR-5F6973 and SWYOR-1AE8AA). Hacksilver jewellery: (e) cut fragment of silver arm-ring from Barmby Moor, East Riding of Yorkshire (PAS-C915EE); (f) cut fragment of silver arm-ring from Spofforth, North Yorkshire (SWYOR-58AFB4). Ingots: (g) and (h) fragment of a silver ingot and complete silver ingot from Weeford, Staffordshire (WMID-C36B61). Note that all of these finds are shown at the same scale for comparison.

**38. Penny of Edward the Elder, 899–924, from Quidenham, Norfolk (NMS-88D191)**
Weight: 1.42 g.

Edward's conquest of the Danelaw with his sister Æthelflaed of Mercia was accompanied by the opening of about a dozen mints, mostly striking in the 'Horizontal/Two-Line' style. Less common are portrait types (with a two-line reverse) and this example from a small hoard of three coins broadly belongs in this group. However, it is lighter than Edward's weight standard of 1.60 g and the reverse inscription makes little sense – numismatists often call this 'blundered' – reading NEIOCR/NEICIO. The coin copies Edward's regular issues, and was probably struck in East Anglia, an area only conquered in 917. It belongs to a group of coins known as the East Anglia portrait type. Quite how it fits in with Edward's regular coinage is uncertain but it was probably struck from late in Edward's reign under his authority but the mints and minting were still under local control, hence adhering to the old Viking weight standard and the presence of blundered legends.

Penny of Edward the Elder from Quidenham, Norfolk (NMS-88D191).

**39. Penny of Athelstan, *c.* 927–39, from Cathedrals, London (LON-6E8535)**
Diameter: 21.2 mm; weight: 1.25 g.

The urbanisation of medieval Britain properly began in the tenth century, based around the network of fortified *burhs* founded from the late ninth century. These developed into towns as foci for craftworking and trade as well as administration. Law codes from Athelstan's (924–39) reign specified that coinage could only be minted in a town and also the number of moneyers who could work in different *burhs*. This continued the expansion of minting across the country and made sure it was well controlled. Two main types were produced from around 927: the 'circumscription cross' with the inscription around a small central cross on both sides and the 'bust crowned' type, to which this coin belongs. It was the first design for centuries to show the king wearing a crown, such a representation related to the display of power. The reverse inscriptions were also consistent, providing information on the moneyer and the mint, here written as GRIMPALD M O LOND C, giving us the name of the moneyer, Grimwald, M O translating as 'moneyer of' and that it was struck at London, the final C for *civitas*, Latin for city. This coin, found opposite the City of London, had not travelled far from the mint before it was lost.

Penny of Athelstan from Cathedrals, London (LON-6E8535).

Penny of Athelstan, 'circumscription cross' type, struck at Canterbury by the moneyer Torhtelm (SUR-825B22).

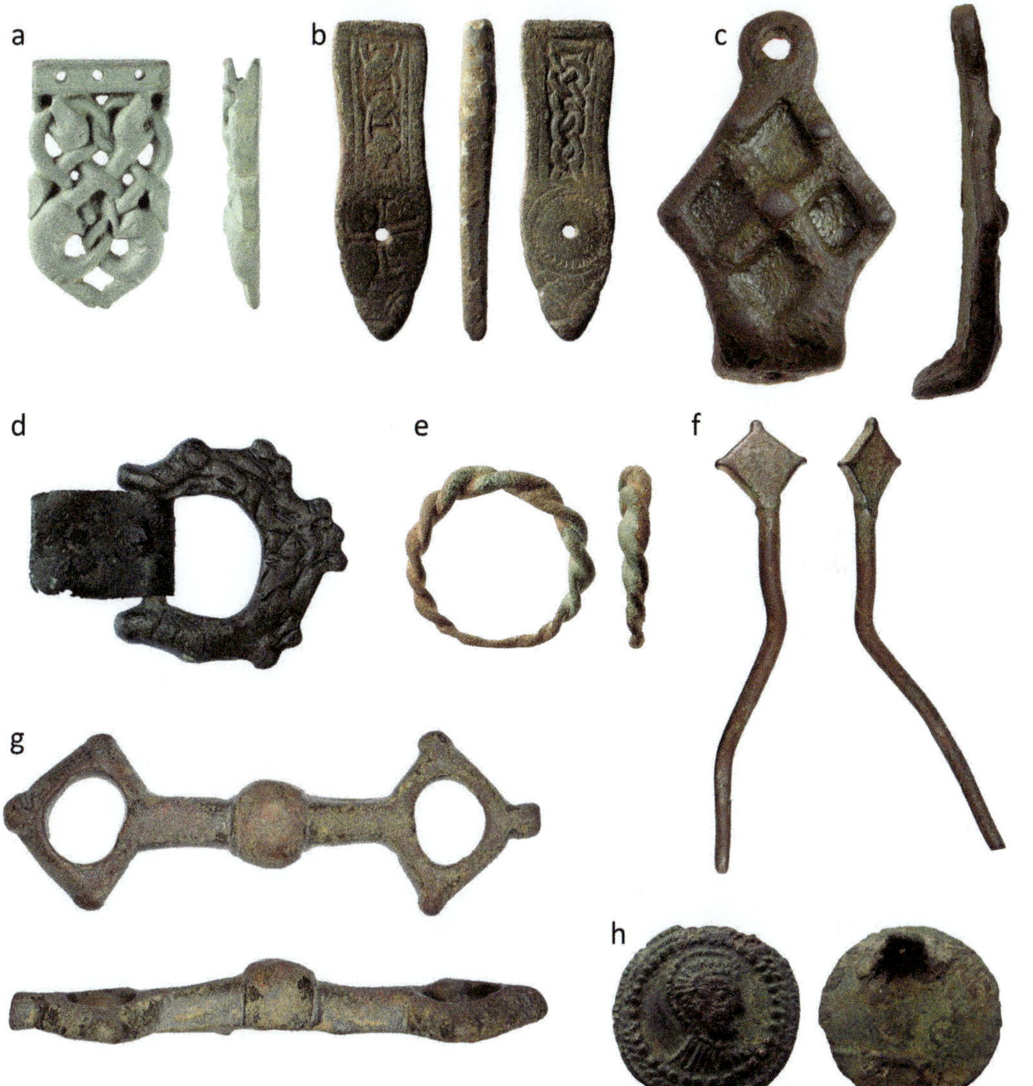


Examples of tenth–eleventh-century craftwork. (a) Winchester-Style strap end (DEV-264F62); (b) Hiberno-Norse strap end (NMS-627136); (c) stirrup-strap mount (GLO-E44626); (d) zoomorphic buckle (DOR-0FB7EB), (e) finger ring (IOW-3AA603); (f) kite-headed pin (YORYM-C3BFBE); (g) harness link (SF-F9C7C2); (h) nummular brooch (FAKL-DFD6D3); (i) cloisonné enamelled brooch (WMID-0074DA); (j) disc brooch with Jellinge Style zoomorphic decoration (WAW-6D8C42). Note that all of these finds are shown at the same scale for comparison.

**40. Penny of Eadwig, 955–9, from Haddiscoe, Norfolk (NMS-5258A8)**
Weight: 0.98 g.

Eadwig's (955–9) short reign was not a happy one, his claim to the throne disputed by Edgar and his supporters, resulting in the division of the kingdom in 957, Eadwig losing land north of the Thames. The coinage was still produced in Eadwig's name, although only four stray finds have been recorded to date by the PAS (plus three coins in the Furness hoard) suggesting generally low levels of coin use for most people. The standardisation in coin design achieved under Athelstan had reverted to regional-based styles again by Eadwig's reign. This 'floral type' has some traits typical from the area between Chester and Gloucester. These include using a rosettes motif and the horizontal inscription on the reverse naming the moneyer, Ælfsige, but not the mint. The odd plant-like motif rising from the centre of the inscription is rarely seen and this is only the second example from Ælfsige to have been found.

Penny of Eadwig from Haddiscoe, Norfolk (NMS-5258A8).

## 41. Penny of Edgar the Peaceful, *c.* 959–73, from St Mary Bourne, Hampshire (HAMP-C4B478)

Dimensions: 21.2x20.1 mm; weight: 1.44 g.

Late in Eadwig's reign Athelstan's 'bust crowned' and 'circumscription cross' types were revived on a limited scale, both continuing into Edgar's reign (959–75). The latter became his main issue prior to reforms in the early 970s, struck across the country at more than twenty-five mints. This is one of very few examples recorded by the PAS. The coin was struck at Winchester (VVINCI) by the moneyer Leofric who was not previously known as a moneyer for this type. Struck on a large flan, the inscriptions are neatly placed within two plain circles, the edge of the die shown by the beaded outer border. The obverse inscription follows Athelstan's coins describing Edgar as REX TO BRIT, 'king of all Britain'.

'Circumscription cross' penny of Edgar from St Mary Bourne, Hampshire (HAMP-C4B478).

'Bust crowned' penny of Edgar, struck by the moneyer Manticen but without a mint named (SF-4159C6).

## 42. Reform penny of Edgar the Peaceful, *c.* 973–5, from Wickenby, Lincolnshire (LIN-299B90)

Around 973 a major reform of the coinage took place under Edgar (959–75). This brought to an end the varied types – and even weights – used in different parts of the country. Uniform designs based on the earlier 'bust crowned' types were introduced, the obverse showing a bust of the king facing left, the reverse a small central cross around which is the name of the moneyer and the mint at which the coin was struck, in this case with the inscription GRIND M-O LINDCOL, literally 'Grind moneyer at Lincoln', an important eleventh-century mint. This reform set the basic standards for minting, which lasted until the reign of Henry II (1154–89). The ramifications of the reforms were important. Dozens of mints were now involved, some big and striking coins throughout and others small and intermittent, but this regional network provided coverage across the country and enabled changes to be introduced quickly, for example when a new king was crowned. The reforms also brought in regular changes of design which helped to maintain a good quality currency in circulation. Its success can be seen in the increased numbers of coins found compared to issues of the tenth century reaching levels not seen since the *sceattas* of the late seventh and early eighth centuries.

Penny of Edgar from Wickenby, Lincolnshire (LIN-299B90).

**43. Penny of Æthelred II, 980s, from West Tytherley, Hampshire (HAMP-26A5F5)**
Diameter: 20 mm; weight: 1.63 g.

The long reign of Æthelred II 'the Unready' (978–1016) saw Edgar's reforms continue with the introduction of regular recoinages, visible in changes to coin design. Renewed Viking activity characterised a difficult reign and he was defeated by the Danish king Swein Forkbeard in 1013 only to regain the throne upon the Dane's death in 1016. This coin belongs to early in Æthelred's reign and was minted at Winchester by Frithemund. Its findspot is not far from the city. The bust design of the obverse continues the overall style of Edgar's coinage, and the inscription ÆÐELRED REX ANGLORX (Æthelred, king of England). The reverse design is new, replacing the small 'circumscription cross' type with a Hand of Providence flanked by an alpha and omega, implying God's blessing on Æthelred's kingship. This is a 'First Hand' type, one of three 'hand' types produced in his reign.

Penny of Æthelred II from West Tytherley, Hampshire (HAMP-26A5F5).

Other types of Æthelred II's 'Hand' issues: Second Hand (SF-63AF63); Benediction Hand (SUR-00CDD2).

Some other coin types of Æthelred II. Top: crux (HAMP-8B9F0D); bottom: long cross (WAW-339A8D).

Top: helmet (IOW-E6CD51); bottom: last small cross (IOW-602BF4).

**44. Cut halfpenny of Æthelred II, *c.* 1003–9, from Burmarsh, Kent (KENT-41B9A6)**
Dimensions: 17.1x8.5 mm; weight: 0.64 g.

Many mint places were involved in coin production from *c.* 973–1066 but over half of the finds recorded by the PAS belong to just eight (London, Lincoln, York, Winchester, Norwich, Thetford, Canterbury and Stamford). With the exception of London, most finds come from the region around each mint. Similar patterns, often represented by just a handful of coin finds, are discernible at smaller mints too. This cut halfpenny of Æthelred II's (978–1016) 'helmet type' was struck at the mint in Dover (Kent) and is one of just ten coins recorded by the PAS to be struck there. All but one of these was found in a coastal location, widely spread from East Sussex to northern Norfolk illustrating how Dover's coinage was dispersed through maritime connections. Only pennies were struck in this period, and this coin has been cut in half to make it a halfpenny; farthings were made by cutting coins into quarters. These cut fractions account for about a third of coin finds dating to 973–1066 recorded by the PAS.

Cut halfpenny of Æthelred II from Burmarsh, Kent (KENT-41B9A6).

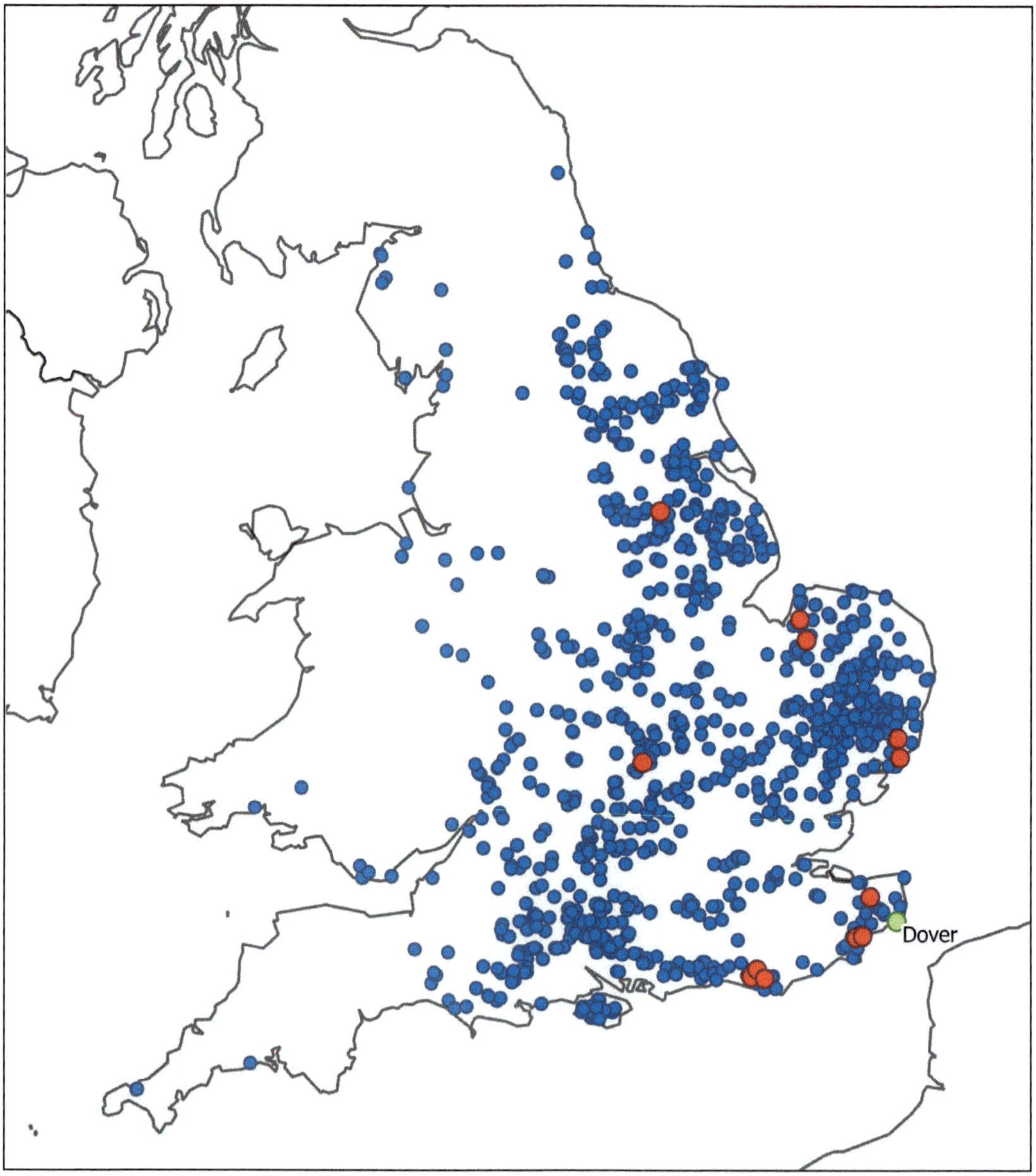


Map showing PAS-recorded finds from the mint at Dover recorded in comparison to all coin finds dating *c.* 973–1066. These coins are shown in red.

## 45. Penny of Cnut, *c.* 1016–early 1020s, from Hook, East Riding of Yorkshire (YORYM-8C2F7A)

Diameter: 19.9 mm; weight: 1 g.

Cnut's (1016–35) conquest of England was not as dramatic as that under William the Conqueror in 1066 but it was nonetheless an important event, bringing a Dane to the throne of England and greater Scandinavian influence overall. The coinage, however, continued to use the system of periodic type changes and the naming of moneyer and mint on all coins. This coin belongs to the earliest of Cnut's issues, the 'quatrefoil' type (named after the shapes on both obverse and reverse) minted until the early 1020s. It was minted by a moneyer called Kolgrimr (COLGRIM on the coin) at York who appears to have moved between Lincoln and York during Æthelred II and Cnut's reign. The king's bust is clear and well defined on this coin with a squat crown and heavily outlined nose, neck and eyebrow, and a raised cheek, all typical of dies from York.

Penny of Cnut from Hook, East Riding of Yorkshire (YORYM-8C2F7A).

A 'pointed helmet' type penny of Cnut, struck by Thurfeth at Thetford (BUC-8275A8).

**46. Lead 'trial piece' of Cnut, mid/late 1020s–*c.* 1035, from Swinbrook and Widford, Oxfordshire (FAJN-351177)**
Dimensions: 22.5x17 mm; weight: 4.74 g.

This bent and torn piece of lead is impressed with the design of a 'short cross' type penny of Cnut (1016–35). The left-facing bust and sceptre on the obverse and central cross on the reverse are reasonably clear but little of the inscription remains, except the letters LVN (for London) on the reverse. Lead strikings are rare and their function is uncertain. Over sixty were found during excavations in London, many dating to the reigns of William I (1066–87) and William II (1087–1100). Often found neatly trimmed they may have been receipts to show customs dues had been paid. This one appears to be a rough, unevenly shaped piece of lead and might instead be a test striking for the dies. Given that it was found so far from London might mean that these dies were used to produce counterfeits, but from what remains it is hard to be sure whether these were official, old or counterfeit dies. If it is a trial piece it gives an interesting glimpse at a rarely seen stage in the minting process.

Lead striking of penny dies of Cnut from Swinbrook and Widford, Oxfordshire (FAJN-351177).

Silver penny of Cnut's 'short cross' type, struck at Thetford by Brunstan (GLO-1CEB74).

**47. Penny of Harold I, late 1030s, from Chalgrave, Bedfordshire (BH-1252E3)**
Diameter: 17 mm; weight: 1.06 g.

Following Cnut's death two of his sons, Harthacnut and Harold Harefoot, claimed succession and it was not until 1037 that Harold was crowned as sole ruler (1037–40; Harthacnut was king from 1040–2). From 1035–7 both struck coins of the same design, generally divided between mints to the south of the Thames using a right-facing bust (Harthacnut) and mints north of the Thames with a left-facing bust (Harold). This coin, a 'jewel cross' type of Harold, was struck by the moneyer Ælfwine at Thetford, which was an important producer of pottery in eastern England. It probably reached Chalgrove via the Icknield Way, which passes through both. Neither ruler's coinage is particularly common as stray finds, fewer than seventy examples currently recorded by the PAS. Their distribution is focused on the area to the south of the line running from the Severn estuary to the Wash, a major contraction compared to those of Cnut for whom far more finds are known from Lincolnshire to the North Yorkshire Moors.

*Above*: Penny of Harold I from Chalgrave, Bedfordshire (BH-1252E3).

*Right*: Cut halfpenny of Harthacnut struck at the Wallingford mint (BUC-2EA283).

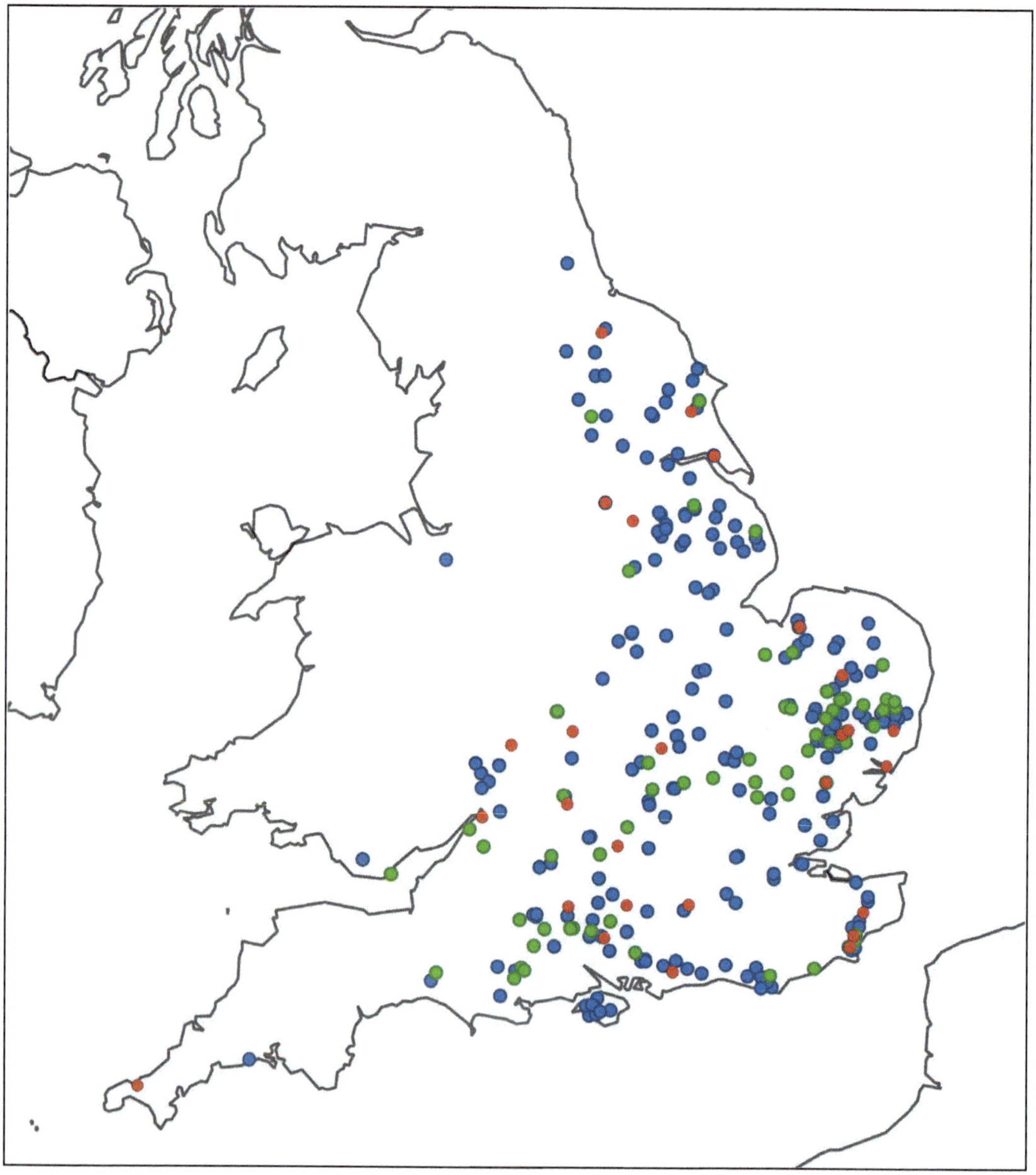

Map showing the distribution of PAS-recorded finds of Cnut (blue dots), Harold I (green dots) and Harthacnut (red dots).

**48. Coin brooch, Edward the Confessor, 1050s, from Nether Wallop, Hampshire (HAMP-oF4407)**
Diameter: 20.4 mm; weight: 2.26 g.

Adapting coins for other uses, often as jewellery, has been seen several times in this book. This coin belongs in a tenth–eleventh-century group of pennies adapted as brooches by adding fittings to the obverse and gilding to the reverse of the coin. Peaking in the mid–late eleventh century, this example is quite typical, using an 'Expanding Cross' type penny of Edward the Confessor (1042–66) dating to the 1050s. That these coin brooches always utilise the cross design on the reverse suggests that they were intended as an expression of Christian identity and were not just jewellery. They are found across the southern half of the country with a defined concentration in the old core of Wessex from Oxfordshire to the south coast and the Isle of Wight. This area accounts for nearly half of the pre-Norman Conquest coin brooches found. The method of adapting coinage into brooches lasted well into the medieval period, with another peak around 1300.

Penny of Edward the Confessor converted into a brooch from Nether Wallop, Hampshire (HAMP-oF4407).

Tenth-century coin brooches. Top: Athelstan (BERK-39FCC8); bottom: Edgar (SUR-8F4A0C).

Eleventh-century coin brooches. Top: Æthelred II (IOW-A6DB92); bottom: Harthacnut (IOW-217104).

**49. Penny of Edward the Confessor, late 1050s, from the Canterbury area, Kent (PUBLIC-A84D86)**
Diameter: 19.5 mm; weight: 1.29 g.

Nearly 400 pennies of Edward the Confessor (1042–66) have been recorded by the PAS, and are found across the country, especially in central, southern and eastern England. Edward's coins are known for the consistency of style in their dies, leading to the suggestion that they were produced in very few workshops. This 'sovereign/eagles' penny of the late 1050s was a major departure in eleventh-century coin design, its complex imagery well preserved on this example from Kent. Struck at Stamford by the moneyer Godwine, it shows the fine detail of the king enthroned, holding a sceptre in one hand and orb with cross in the other, a design influenced by Edward's seal of *c.* 1052. The birds in the cross arms on the reverse are interpreted as eagles, although their meaning is unknown.

Penny of Edward the Confessor from the Canterbury area, Kent (PUBLIC-A84D86).

PAS-recorded types of Edward the Confessor. Top row: PACX (BERK-359737); radiate/small cross (YORYM-BA59C9). Row 2: trefoil quadrilateral (WILT-7548C1); small flan (OXON-B762F7). Row 3: expanding cross (SF-E3AADB); pointed helmet (BH-06685E). Row 4: hammer cross (BERK-1536EB); bust facing (WMID-69B593). Row 5: transitional pyramids (WAW-F86AD7); pyramids (SWYOR-1158AD).

**50. Penny of Harold II, 1066, from Westborough and Dry Doddington, Lincolnshire (DENO-E3DCE5)**
Diameter: 19.6 mm; weight: 1.27 g.

Harold II only ruled for the ten months from January–October 1066 before his death at the Battle of Hastings. Harold's 'PAX' type was his only issue, the word PAX displayed across the centre of coin and meaning 'peace' in Latin. Edward the Confessor also started his reign with a 'PAX' coin and it was probably meant to relay the wealth and stability of the kingdom. Harold's coins are not uncommon given the brevity of his reign, and were produced at forty-eight mints showing the capacity of the eleventh-century state. This coin was struck by the moneyer Forna at Nottingham. The obverse shows a left-facing bust of Harold with well-defined, somewhat chiselled features. His death and the accession of William I 'the Conqueror' brought a new dynasty to the throne, the Normans.

Penny of Harold II from Westborough and Dry Doddington, Lincolnshire (DENO-E3DCE5).

Penny of William the Conqueror, struck at Winchester by the moneyer Lifinc (LEIC-6CEBD0). The bust style is very similar to Harold II's.

# Further Reading

This book was written using many references and it is impossible to include all of them here. For good introductions to the archaeology, history and numismatics of the period see:


Fleming, Robin, *Britain After Rome: The Fall and Rise, 400–1070* (London: Penguin, 2011).

Gannon, Anna, *The Iconography of Early Anglo-Saxon Coinage* (Oxford: Oxford University Press, 2003)

Hamerow, Helena, *Rural Settlements and Society in Anglo-Saxon England* (Oxford: Oxford University Press, 2012).

Higham, Nicholas and Ryan, Martin, *The Anglo-Saxon World* (London: Yale University Press, 2013).

Hinton, David, *Gilt and Gold, Pots and Pins: Possessions and People in Medieval Britain* (Oxford: Oxford University Press, 2005).

Loveluck, Christopher, *Northwest Europe in the Early Middle Ages, c. AD 600–1150: A Comparative Archaeology* (Cambridge: Cambridge University Press, 2013).

Naismith, Rory, *Money and Power in Anglo-Saxon England: the Southern English Kingdoms 757–865* (Cambridge: Cambridge University Press, 2012)

Naismith, Rory, *Medieval European Coinage 8: Britain and Ireland c. 400–1066* (Cambridge: Cambridge University Press, 2017)


Academic papers on early medieval coinage and archaeology also appear regularly in journals including the *British Numismatic Journal* and *Medieval Archaeology.* Important projects and research are often summarised in magazines such as *Current Archaeology and British Archaeology.*

## Images

The images in this book are not reproduced to scale. Where listed in the record, dimensions for each find are provided in the individual entry.